"In *Turn Your Eyes*, Winfree and Sharonda skillfully walk us through the Psalms, widening our perspective on God's work in and around our lives. Done with careful exposition and thoughtfulness, this Bible study will lead you to marvel at God's glory and grace."
   Emily A. Jensen and Laura Wifler, coauthors, *Risen Motherhood* and *Gospel Mom*

"This accessible Bible study centers a group to marinate in the beauty and richness of the Psalms. The content invites participants to look up to God's presence and power and then look out as they study, share insights, and sing his goodness in the context of community."
   Karen Hodge, Coordinator of Women's Ministries, Presbyterian Church in America; coauthor, *Transformed: Life-Taker to Life-Giver* and *Life-Giving Leadership*

"The Bible's songbook can feel intimidating to study with its imagery and poetic devices, but if we skip the Psalms, we miss so much about God's good character. What I love about *Turn Your Eyes* is that Winfree and Sharonda guide you through a study of the Psalms by teaching you *how* to study these songs. You'll learn how to observe, interpret, and apply the Psalms as you work through this study, and you'll be equipped to gaze on God's goodness every time you open your Bible."
   Glenna Marshall, author, *The Promise Is His Presence*; *Everyday Faithfulness*; and *Memorizing Scripture*

"*Turn Your Eyes* is a theologically rich study that empowers readers to engage the Psalms with clarity and confidence. By unpacking the context, structure, and literary style of each type of psalm, it equips readers with the essential tools they need to uncover the timeless wisdom hidden within these sacred songs. Whether you're new to Bible study or seeking to go deeper, this resource will help you connect with the Psalms in a way that is both inspiring and spiritually transformative."
   Elizabeth Woodson, Bible teacher; author, *Live Free*; *From Beginning to Forever*; and *Embrace Your Life*

"There's a reason God's people run to the Psalms in distress. In these songs, we find language for the many things we experience in life. But studying them can be a challenge because they don't follow a linear pattern. In *Turn Your Eyes*, Winfree Brisley and Sharonda Cooper give a framework for studying the Psalms thematically and practically. I've long wanted a study on the Psalms to give to friends. This is it! If you want to read the Psalms with fresh eyes, this study is for you—and your friends."
   Courtney Reissig, author, *Teach Me to Feel: Worshiping Through the Psalms in Every Season of Life*

Turn Your Eyes

Turn Your Eyes

A Bible Study on the Psalms

Winfree Brisley and Sharonda Cooper

WHEATON, ILLINOIS

Turn Your Eyes: A Bible Study on the Psalms

© 2025 by Winfree Brisley and Sharonda Cooper

Published by Crossway
        1300 Crescent Street
        Wheaton, Illinois 60187

All rights reserved. No part of this publication may be reproduced, stored in a retrieval system, or transmitted in any form by any means, electronic, mechanical, photocopy, recording, or otherwise, without the prior permission of the publisher, except as provided for by USA copyright law. Crossway® is a registered trademark in the United States of America.

Cover design: Dan Farrell

Cover image: Lynne Millar

First printing 2025

Printed in China

Scripture quotations are from the ESV® Bible (The Holy Bible, English Standard Version®), © 2001 by Crossway, a publishing ministry of Good News Publishers. Used by permission. All rights reserved. The ESV text may not be quoted in any publication made available to the public by a Creative Commons license. The ESV may not be translated in whole or in part into any other language.

All emphases in Scripture quotations have been added by the authors.

Trade paperback ISBN: 978-1-4335-9858-6

ePub ISBN: 978-1-4335-9860-9

PDF ISBN: 978-1-4335-9859-3

Crossway is a publishing ministry of Good News Publishers.

RRD			34	33	32	31	30	29	28	27	26	25
15	14	13	12	11	10	9	8	7	6	5	4	3	2	1

To my parents, thank you for teaching me to love God's word and read it every day.
Winfree Brisley

To Rob, thank you for making it possible for me to follow my every calling.
To Sydney and Renne, being your mom is the best job ever. Keep turning
your eyes to Jesus until we are standing side-by-side in his presence.
Sharonda Cooper

ABOUT THE COVER ARTWORK

The artwork featured on the cover of this study is an original oil painting by Lynne Millar, an accomplished artist working in California. Painting is her way of paying attention to and processing the beauty and complexity of the world through color, brushstroke, and texture.

In this work there is a strong sense of movement that draws the eye from bottom to top and dark to bright. As the blush petals unfold, they reach out for the sunlight. This study invites us to follow the example of these flowers by turning our eyes toward God as our source of life: "For with you is the fountain of life; in your light do we see light" (Ps. 36:9).

Contents

Introduction   *1*
Winfree Brisley

Week 1: How to Study the Psalms (Psalm 18)   7
Winfree Brisley

Week 2: Turn to God for Wisdom (Psalms 1 and 73)   *39*
Sharonda Cooper

Week 3: Turn to God with Thanksgiving (Psalms 34 and 107)   67
Sharonda Cooper

Week 4: Turn to God in Repentance (Psalms 51 and 53)   97
Winfree Brisley

Week 5: Turn to God in Suffering (Psalms 102 and 74)   *125*
Winfree Brisley

Week 6: Turn to God as King (Psalms 72 and 110)   *155*
Sharonda Cooper

Week 7: Turn to God in Trust (Psalms 27 and 16)   *183*
Winfree Brisley

Week 8: Turn to God in Praise (Psalms 46 and 84)   *213*
Sharonda Cooper

Appendix: Questions for Studying Additional Psalms   *241*

Introduction

Some years ago, I hiked the seaside trails of Cinque Terre, Italy, on a vacation with friends. The trails connect five cliffside villages overlooking the Mediterranean Sea, and they offer spectacular views. But for the first part of our hike, the only scenery I saw was the path in front of my feet. The terrain was rugged with rocks and roots and narrow passes, so I focused on putting one foot safely in front of the other.

Eventually though, the path widened and there was space to step aside and take in the view. As I lifted my gaze and turned my eyes out over the sea, the beauty almost took my breath away. I remember telling my friends that if the fallen earth could be so beautiful, I couldn't imagine the glory to come in the new heaven and earth. My heart swelled in worship of the great God who created such beauty—and my perspective on the hike was transformed.

Sure, I still wanted to make it to the next village without falling over a cliff, but I remembered that the hike wasn't just about getting from one place to another. I kept turning my eyes to take in the beauty. I kept turning my attention to enjoy the conversation. And by the end, though my body was exhausted, my spirit was refreshed.

I don't know about you, but sometimes I walk through life the way I started that hike. I'm just keeping my head down, putting one foot in front of the other, so focused on what's right in front of me that I miss the bigger picture of God's work in me and his glory around me. If only I would turn my eyes, if only I would catch a glimpse of the beauty and glory of the Lord, my heart would turn to worship and my perspective on my circumstances might be changed.

As the old hymn "Turn Your Eyes upon Jesus" encourages us,

> O soul, are you weary and troubled?
> No light in the darkness you see?
> There's light for a look at the Savior,
> And life more abundant and free.
>
> Turn your eyes upon Jesus,
> Look full in his wonderful face,
> And the things of earth will grow strangely dim,
> In the light of his glory and grace.[1]

If you're like me, you might be thinking, *Yes—I need that! But how can I practically turn my eyes to Jesus?* There are many ways, but the Psalms are a good place to start. Page after page, we find the psalmists turning to the Lord, telling him about their tragedies and their triumphs, asking him for help with decisions and doubts, confessing their sin and resting in his salvation. There are 150 psalms, and they engage every condition and circumstance of life.

But the Psalms aren't just in the Bible to show us that others have shared our emotions and experiences. They're divided into five books because we're meant to connect them with the Pentateuch—the first five books of the Old Testament, sometimes called the *Torah* or *the books of Moses*. The five books of the Pentateuch were written for our instruction (in fact, *torah* means "instruction"), to help us understand the story of redemption.[2]

---

1   Helen Howarth Lemmel, "Turn Your Eyes upon Jesus," 1922, https://hymnary.org.
2   Nancy Guthrie, interview with Mark Futato, *Help Me Teach the Bible*, podcast, March 18, 2018, https://www .thegospelcoalition.org.

Likewise, the five books of the Psalms were written for our instruction. They teach us how to bring our emotions and experiences—all of life—to God, so our lives are transformed by his presence and wisdom.

Whatever path you're on as you come to this study—whether you're strolling down easy street, stuck in the mud, or staring at a crossroads and unsure which way to go; whether you're weeping, rejoicing, or questioning—let me invite you to turn your eyes upon Jesus, to take a look at the Savior in the pages of the Psalms. Our circumstances may not change, but we'll begin to see them in the light of God's glory and grace. And as we do, I pray we'll find life more abundant and free.

How to Use This Study

Whether you've never read the Bible, have studied the Bible for years, or are somewhere in between, we've designed this study to help you grow in your understanding of the Psalms and how they apply to your everyday life. As you might have guessed, since there are 150 psalms, we won't be able to study each one in just eight weeks. But we will be able to study each major type of psalm: wisdom, thanksgiving, lament, kingship, trust, and praise.

We'll spend the first week learning characteristics of psalms in general, and then over the following seven weeks, we'll study two psalms from each category each week. Our weekly rhythm will consist of observing, interpreting, and applying each passage of Scripture over the course of five days of study.

Day 1 will be *observation* for the first psalm of the week—reading the passage and asking the question: *What does the text say*? We'll pay attention to details like repeated words and main ideas. And we'll begin to move into *interpretation*, asking: *What does the text mean?* We'll consider aspects like figurative language and poetic structure and how they convey the psalmist's message.

Day 2 will move deeper into *interpretation* of the first psalm of the week. We'll read the passage again and continue to consider what it means by exploring its larger context in the rest of the Bible. Does it relate to an Old Testament story or prophecy? Is it quoted in the New Testament? How might it point to Christ? And how do these connections help us understand the text? As we come to understand what the text means, we'll move into *application*, asking: *How can I faithfully respond?* In light of the truths we glean about the nature of humanity and the character of God, we'll consider what it might mean for these truths to transform what we think, feel, and do.

Day 3 will follow the same pattern as Day 1, seeking to observe and interpret the second psalm of the week.

Day 4 will follow the same pattern as Day 2, seeking to interpret and apply the second psalm of the week.

Each week will end on **Day 5** with a *reflection*. After reading it, you'll find a few questions to help you reflect on what you've learned that week.

Please plan on approximately twenty minutes of study each day (or 1.5 hours each week). We recommend you have an actual Bible in front of you, rather than using an app on your phone or computer. You'll need it for cross-referencing verses, and a physical copy helps you more readily see the passage in its context. The provided Bible passages in this study are from the English Standard Version, but feel free to use a different translation.

Prayer

At the beginning of each week, you'll find a section called "Turn to God in Prayer." These prayers will include verses from various psalms to help you practice praying the Psalms. You can use the prayer provided or pray with your own words. Either way, we encourage you to take time to ask God to meet you as you study his living and active word.

Memory Work

A memory verse(s) is also provided at the beginning of each week and reprinted at the end of each day of study. Spend a few minutes each day working on memorizing it. The discipline of hiding God's word in your heart will bear much fruit in your life and the lives of those around you.

Discussion Questions

At the end of each chapter, you'll find a list of questions for group discussion. These are based on the work you've done throughout the week. There is a fun "icebreaker" question and a "warm-up" question. Both are intended to be quick and easy ways to get the group talking. Keep the answers to these short so you have plenty of time to dig into the text together.

Hymn for the Week

Each week will close with a hymn that relates to the psalm(s) studied that week. You might sing it on your own or with your group, listen to a recording of it, or use the lyrics as a prompt for prayer and meditation.

Videos

We hope to provide videos of the keynote teaching sessions from TGCW26 (The Gospel Coalition Women's 2026 conference). Each video will align with the chapters and, Lord willing, will be available after the conference in June 2026 on the TGC website (https://www.thegospelcoalition.org/).

As you turn your eyes to the Lord through the Psalms, may you come to see all seasons and circumstances of life in the light of his glory and grace.

Week 1

How to Study the Psalms

Psalm 18

You may have heard the Psalms referred to as the songbook of the Bible. Don't worry if you're not musically inclined—there's no singing required for this study! But knowing the Psalms were written to be sung informs how we read them. Just as we wouldn't read song lyrics the same way we read a novel or an email, we can't read psalms the same way we read narratives and letters in the Bible.

So this first week of study will be unique—we're going to walk through Psalm 18 as an example of how to study the Psalms. We'll learn some technical terms, consider how various features of the Psalms impact our understanding, and begin to interpret and apply the text. On days 1-4, we'll explore one aspect of Psalm 18 each day that will help us know what to look for in the other psalms we study. As we turn our eyes to the text this week, I pray we'll begin to catch a glimpse of God's glory and grace in the pages of the Psalms.

🔼 Turn to God in Prayer

Father, thank you for giving us your word so we can know you and turn to you with all our emotions and experiences. Please "open my eyes, that I may behold wondrous things out of your law" this week (Ps. 119:18). By the help of your Spirit, "turn my eyes from looking at worthless things, and give me life in your ways" (Ps. 119:37). In Jesus's name, amen.

💙 Memory Verse

> In my distress I called upon the Lord;
> to my God I cried for help.
> From his temple he heard my voice,
> and my cry to him reached his ears. (Ps. 18:6)

LOOK FOR POETIC DEVICES

Psalm 18

The Lord Is My Rock and My Fortress

To the choirmaster. A Psalm of David, the servant of the Lord, who addressed the words of this song to the Lord on the day when the Lord delivered him from the hand of all his enemies, and from the hand of Saul. He said:

¹ I love you, O Lord, my strength.
² The Lord is my rock and my fortress
   and my deliverer,
  my God, my rock, in whom I take
   refuge,
  my shield, and the horn of my
   salvation, my stronghold.
³ I call upon the Lord, who is worthy to
   be praised,
  and I am saved from my enemies.

4   The cords of death encompassed me;
        the torrents of destruction assailed me;
 5   the cords of Sheol entangled me;
        the snares of death confronted me.

 6   In my distress I called upon the LORD;
        to my God I cried for help.
     From his temple he heard my voice,
        and my cry to him reached his ears.

 7   Then the earth reeled and rocked;
        the foundations also of the mountains trembled
        and quaked, because he was angry.
 8   Smoke went up from his nostrils,
        and devouring fire from his mouth;
        glowing coals flamed forth from him.
 9   He bowed the heavens and came down;
        thick darkness was under his feet.
 10 He rode on a cherub and flew;
        he came swiftly on the wings of the wind.
 11 He made darkness his covering, his canopy around him,
        thick clouds dark with water.
 12 Out of the brightness before him
        hailstones and coals of fire broke through his clouds.

 13 The LORD also thundered in the heavens,
        and the Most High uttered his voice,
        hailstones and coals of fire.
 14 And he sent out his arrows and scattered them;
        he flashed forth lightnings and routed them.
 15 Then the channels of the sea were seen,
        and the foundations of the world were laid bare

at your rebuke, O Lord,
    at the blast of the breath of your nostrils.

16 He sent from on high, he took me;
    he drew me out of many waters.
17 He rescued me from my strong enemy
    and from those who hated me,
    for they were too mighty for me.
18 They confronted me in the day of my calamity,
    but the Lord was my support.
19 He brought me out into a broad place;
    he rescued me, because he delighted in me.

20 The Lord dealt with me according to my righteousness;
    according to the cleanness of my hands he rewarded me.
21 For I have kept the ways of the Lord,
    and have not wickedly departed from my God.
22 For all his rules were before me,
    and his statutes I did not put away from me.
23 I was blameless before him,
    and I kept myself from my guilt.
24 So the Lord has rewarded me according to my righteousness,
    according to the cleanness of my hands in his sight.

25 With the merciful you show yourself merciful;
    with the blameless man you show yourself blameless;
26 with the purified you show yourself pure;
    and with the crooked you make yourself seem tortuous.
27 For you save a humble people,
    but the haughty eyes you bring down.
28 For it is you who light my lamp;
    the Lord my God lightens my darkness.

29 For by you I can run against a troop,
  and by my God I can leap over a wall.
30 This God—his way is perfect;
  the word of the LORD proves true;
  he is a shield for all those who take refuge in him.

31 For who is God, but the LORD?
  And who is a rock, except our God?—
32 the God who equipped me with strength
  and made my way blameless.
33 He made my feet like the feet of a deer
  and set me secure on the heights.
34 He trains my hands for war,
  so that my arms can bend a bow of bronze.
35 You have given me the shield of your salvation,
  and your right hand supported me,
  and your gentleness made me great.
36 You gave a wide place for my steps under me,
  and my feet did not slip.
37 I pursued my enemies and overtook them,
  and did not turn back till they were consumed.
38 I thrust them through, so that they were not able to rise;
  they fell under my feet.
39 For you equipped me with strength for the battle;
  you made those who rise against me sink under me.
40 You made my enemies turn their backs to me,
  and those who hated me I destroyed.
41 They cried for help, but there was none to save;
  they cried to the LORD, but he did not answer them.
42 I beat them fine as dust before the wind;
  I cast them out like the mire of the streets.

43 You delivered me from strife with the people;
    you made me the head of the nations;
    people whom I had not known served me.
44 As soon as they heard of me they obeyed me;
    foreigners came cringing to me.
45 Foreigners lost heart
    and came trembling out of their fortresses.

46 The LORD lives, and blessed be my rock,
    and exalted be the God of my salvation—
47 the God who gave me vengeance
    and subdued peoples under me,
48 who rescued me from my enemies;
    yes, you exalted me above those who rose against me;
    you delivered me from the man of violence.

49 For this I will praise you, O LORD, among the nations,
    and sing to your name.
50 Great salvation he brings to his king,
    and shows steadfast love to his anointed,
    to David and his offspring forever.

The Psalms have a unique way of engaging our emotions. They convey various tones with great depth of feeling and help us pour out our hearts when we don't know what to say. How do they do all that?

While many parts of the Bible are written in prose, the Psalms are Hebrew poetry. In poetry, ideas are conveyed with artistry and beauty, through figurative language and careful arrangement of words. So we pay attention not only to *what* is said but to *how* it's said. Let's turn to Psalm 18 and look for some poetic features commonly used in the Psalms.

Begin by reading all of Psalm 18, and then answer the following questions focused on verses 1–6.

1. Many Psalms have a title and a superscription (a brief note that may include musical instructions, the type of psalm, the author's name, and/or the psalm's context). You'll find these above the first verse.

   What is the title of Psalm 18?

   _____

   _____

   What information do we learn from the superscription?

   Who wrote this psalm?

   _____

   Why did he write it?

   _____

2. What is David's tone in verses 1–6? How does he seem to feel?

   _____

   _____

   _____

   _____

As we mentioned in the introduction, there are different types of psalms. Psalm 18 is a psalm of thanksgiving, and in these opening verses, David expresses his gratitude to the Lord using the two primary features of Hebrew poetry: imagery and parallelism. *Imagery* uses words to create a mental picture and convey an impression of someone or something. *Parallelism* emphasizes an idea by saying the same thing in slightly different ways, as we see in verse 2.

Read verses 1–3 again, paying particular attention to the imagery.

3. List all the words David uses to describe God in verses 1–2.

4. David primarily uses these descriptions figuratively. While "deliverer" directly describes what God has done for David (and even more so, for Israel when he delivered them out of Egypt), we know that God is not literally a rock, a fortress, or a shield. So, let's consider what David is trying to convey about God.

What are the characteristics of a rock? What might the image of a rock suggest about God's nature and character?

What are fortresses and shields used for? What do these images convey about what God has done for David?

5. Hebrew poetry also uses parallelism. As you look at a psalm, you'll see that most verses are divided into two or more lines. Parallelism refers to the relationship between these lines.

For example, notice how the circled words in the first line of verse 2 are directly repeated in the second line to add emphasis.

> The LORD is my rock and my fortress and my deliverer,
>   my God, my rock, in whom I take refuge,
>   my shield, and the horn of my salvation, my stronghold.

The second and third lines also use similar, but slightly different, words to help us grasp the fuller meaning of the first line. How do the underlined descriptions help you understand what David means when he calls God his fortress and deliverer?

6. In verses 4–5, David repeats the same idea in four different ways, changing the imagery slightly each time.

List the different words/phrases that describe what was threatening David.

Why might David have described death, rather than Saul, as threatening him?

From the superscription we know that David's enemy Saul was trying to kill him. God had anointed David to be the new king of Israel, but Saul was the reigning king—and he wasn't going down without a fight. However, David personifies death generally, rather than Saul specifically, as threatening him. While he's writing this psalm in the context of a specific situation, he's also pointing to larger truths about the nature of man and the character of God.

Saul was a serious foe, but death was a greater enemy for David—and for us. When Adam and Eve sinned against God in the garden of Eden, death entered the world. Now all of us are born sinful, and death is the just punishment for our sin. But David doesn't just want us to understand our enemy; he wants us to look to our deliverer.

7. In verse 6, we find two pairs of parallel lines that explain how David responded to the threat of death and how God responded to David.

"In [his] distress," what did David do?

_____

_____

"From his temple," what did God do?

_____

_____

If I were to summarize verses 1–6, I might say this: David praises God for rescuing him from death. But I imagine you wouldn't find my version as compelling as David's. You likely wouldn't feel a connection to your own life or be compelled to do anything.

When we read David's poetic descriptions, however, our minds can imagine the danger, and our hearts can feel the security he finds in the Lord. We feel

HOW TO STUDY THE PSALMS 17

it in such a way that we too want to cry out to God, having confidence he will hear our voices as he has heard David's. Close this time in prayer, asking the Lord for help in your struggles (great or small) and resting in him as your rock and refuge.

💙 Memory Verse

In my distress I called upon the LORD;
    to my God I cried for help.
From his temple he heard my voice,
    and my cry to him reached his ears. (Ps. 18:6)

LOOK FOR CONTEXT

If you've been in a group setting where someone told an inside joke, you can probably appreciate the importance of context. When you don't know the backstory, a comment that sends others into side-splitting laughter can leave you confused.

Today, we'll see how context can be important in understanding the Psalms. Sometimes, the psalmists refer to events recorded in other parts of Scripture, and for us to understand the psalm, we need to know the backstory.

Read Psalm 18:7–24 and then answer the questions below.

1. In verses 7–15, David describes how God answered his cry for help.

    What are some images that help you visualize God coming to David's rescue?

18 HOW TO STUDY THE PSALMS

List any images you find confusing or surprising.

2. Verses 8–9 use a type of figurative language called *anthropomorphism* (a fun term to throw out at your next social gathering!), which describes God using human characteristics even though he doesn't have a physical body.

What physical attributes are ascribed to God?

God is a spirit—he doesn't literally have these features. Why might David want us to think of God in physical terms as we imagine his rescue?

As far as we know, David didn't experience the scene he describes—it's a poetic representation of God's deliverance. So how can we understand the imagery? Thankfully, David left us some clues that point to other passages in the Old Testament.

3. Read Exodus 19:16–20, where God comes to make a covenant with his people (represented by Moses) at Mount Sinai. List images you find that are similar to David's descriptions in Psalm 18:7–11.

HOW TO STUDY THE PSALMS · 19

4. Read Joshua 10:10–11, where God delivers his people (led by Joshua) from their enemy, the Amorites. What similarities do you see between this story and Psalm 18:12–14?

5. Exodus 15 records the song of Moses after God delivered his people from slavery in Egypt by parting the Red Sea to enable their escape. Read Exodus 15:8, and list the descriptions that correspond to David's imagery in Psalm 18:15.

Yesterday, we noted that David described himself as "the servant of the LORD" in the superscription. That particular phrase is only used to describe three men in the Old Testament: Moses, Joshua, and David.[1] In Psalm 18:7–15, we've seen how David draws on stories of God delivering his people through Moses and Joshua.

6. By explaining his own deliverance as one example among many where God delivers his people, what do you think David wants us to understand about God?

---

1 James M. Hamilton Jr., *Psalms Volume 1* (Lexham Academic, 2021), 239.

David identifies himself with Joshua battling the Amorites and Moses fleeing Egypt as if to say, *The same God who delivered them from their enemies, delivered me.* David connects himself to Moses at Mount Sinai as if to say, *The same covenant promises God made to his people at Mount Sinai, God made to me.*[2] David doesn't want us to focus on the particular details of how God rescued him on one occasion. David wants us to see the pattern of how God faithfully delivers his people time and time again.

7. In verses 17–19, David summarizes what God has done for him.

Which phrase from verse 17 is repeated in verse 19?

Why does David say God rescued him (vv. 17 and 19)?

Before we move on, let's remember that the Psalms weren't primarily written to be read. They were written to be sung and prayed—by all God's people. David means for us to say along with him, "God rescued me because he delighted in me."

8. We aren't often in situations as dire as David's, but we all face challenges that seem "too mighty" for us to handle.

---

2   Nancy Guthrie, interview with James Hamilton, *Help Me Teach the Bible*, podcast, November 1, 2018, https://www.thegospelcoalition.org.

What sort of difficulty are you facing today?

How does verse 19 encourage you to cry out to God for help?

We serve a God who has been faithful to help his people generation after generation. He rescued Moses, Joshua, and David—and he rescues us too.

💙 Memory Verse

> In my distress I called upon the LORD;
>   to my God I cried for help.
> From his temple he heard my voice,
>   and my cry to him reached his ears. (Ps. 18:6)

LOOK FOR STRUCTURE

When we read a fiction book, we expect it to follow a predictable structure—a conflict builds up to a climax and then is somehow resolved by the end of the story. When we read a nonfiction text, we expect the writer to build an argument using supporting details that bring us to a logical conclusion. Knowing how a text is structured gives us clues about how to understand it.

Likewise, as we study the Psalms, we need to consider how the author organized his ideas in order to understand his larger point. Today, we'll learn about one of the common poetic structures used in the Psalms.

Read Psalm 18:20–30 and then answer the questions that follow.

1. David begins and ends the first section of today's text with almost identical verses. What characteristics of himself does David highlight in verses 20 and 24?

2. List details from verses 21 and 23 that help us understand what David means when he refers to his "righteousness" (doing what is right[3]) and the "cleanness of his hands."

Verse 21:

Verse 23:

David says he has followed the Lord's ways and kept the Lord's rules, even going so far as to call himself "blameless" before God. If you're familiar with David's

---

3 Carl Ellis, "Biblical Righteousness Is a Four-Paned Window," The Gospel Coalition, August 22, 2018, https://www.thegospelcoalition.org.

HOW TO STUDY THE PSALMS 23

life, you probably know he had some famous failures—adultery and murder among them. So how can we make sense of verses 20–24?

Since the first and last verses of this section are almost identical, we have a clue about how David structured the section. In many parts of the Bible, including the Psalms, biblical authors use what's called *chiastic structure* to organize their ideas. Chiastic structure is like a sandwich meant to highlight the meat in the middle (see below). A chiasm presents a series of ideas in a sequence and then repeats them in opposite order to create a mirror reflection. Generally, the most important idea, the meat in our sandwich analogy, is placed at the *center* of a chiasm (in this case verse 22), and it helps us understand the other parts.

The chiastic structure of verses 20–24 looks like this:[4]

Verse 20: God rewarded David because of his righteousness and clean hands. (*Bread*)
   Verse 21: David kept the ways of the Lord. (*Cheese*)
      Verse 22: David continually looked to God's rules and statutes. (*Meat*)
   Verse 23: David kept himself from sin. (*Cheese*)
Verse 24: God rewarded David because of his righteousness and clean hands. (*Bread*)

3. What does verse 22 suggest as the reason for David's righteousness?

4 Hamilton, *Psalms Volume 1*, 244.

4. Why do you think keeping God's word in front of him helped David keep the ways of the Lord?

As Dr. James Hamilton, a Bible commentator and seminary professor, explains, "David is not righteous in and of himself."[5] Rather, "by faith in [God's] word David's character has been shaped by and conformed to [God's character]."[6] Chiastic structure helps us see that the most important idea in these verses is not that David is righteous—it's that God's word produced righteousness in David.

And verses 20–24 aren't the only place in Psalm 18 where David used chiastic structure. A larger chiastic structure organizes the entire Psalm:[7]

> Verse 1–6: David in Danger
> > Verses 7–19: God in Action
> > > Verses 20–24: The Character of David
> > > Verses 25–30: The Character of God
> > Verses 31–45: David in Conquest
> Verses 46–50: David in Praise

At the center of this larger chiasm, we find the two sections we're studying today. Together, they will help us understand the psalm's main idea.

---

5   Hamilton, *Psalms Volume 1*, 243.
6   Hamilton, *Psalms Volume 1*, 246.
7   Hamilton, *Psalms Volume 1*, 230.

5. Read verses 25–30, paying attention to how David describes God's character.

What does God do for "humble people" (v. 27)?

How does God help "all those who take refuge in him" (v. 30)?

6. Why do you think David proclaims of God, "his way is *perfect*" (v. 30)? How is this description different from David's descriptions of his own righteousness in verses 20–24?

In verses 25–30, we find a general principle that God honors those who honor him. He saves the humble; he rescues the righteous. But remember, we learned in verses 20–24 that David wasn't righteous on his own. No matter how many commands we obey, we are all sinful and fall short of God's perfect glory and righteousness (Rom. 3:23). It's only by Jesus's perfect obedience that we can be made completely righteous (Rom. 5:19).

At the center of Psalm 18, we find a glorious truth—God is not only the one who rescues the righteous (vv. 25–30); he's the one who makes us righteous (vv. 20–24).

7. As we, like David, come to God's word in faith, the Holy Spirit conforms us more and more into the righteous image of Jesus Christ.

What's an area of your life where you need to turn from sin and ask God to help you grow in righteousness?

_____

_____

What's one practical change you can make to keep God's word before you?

_____

_____

 Memory Verse

> In my distress I called upon the LORD;
>   to my God I cried for help.
> From his temple he heard my voice,
>   and my cry to him reached his ears. (Ps. 18:6)

LOOK FOR CHRIST

It may seem odd to have a day dedicated to looking for Christ in the Psalms. Jesus doesn't come on the scene until the New Testament, right? Well, yes and no. It's true, we don't find the name Jesus in the Old Testament. But in one way or another, the Son of God, the second person of the Trinity, is in every story and passage of the Bible—including the Psalms.

Today we'll see that Psalm 18 isn't just about King David—it points forward to the true King,

Jesus Christ. Finding shadows of Jesus in these verses will help train our eyes to look for him in the other psalms we'll study.

Read Psalm 18:31–50, and then answer the questions below.

1. In verses 32–36, David explains how God equipped him for battle in two ways: physically and spiritually.

   What are some ways God equipped David physically? (See verses 32–34 and 36.)

   In verses 32 and 35, how does David say God equipped him spiritually?

2. In verse 39, David says that because God equipped him for battle, he was able to defeat his enemies.

   What happened to David's enemies according to verses 37–42?

   As you read this section, what emotions stir in you?

3. In particular, verse 41 can pull at our heartstrings as we consider how it contrasts with verse 6. When David cried out to the Lord, the Lord heard and came to rescue. But when David's enemies cried out to the Lord, "he did not answer them." Why might God have answered David but not his enemies?

4. In verses 49–50, David includes some easily overlooked—but very important—details that help us understand the nature of God's love and salvation. According to verse 50:

Whom does God bring salvation to?

Whom does God show steadfast love to?

The word "anointed" refers to the practice of anointing a new king's head with oil at his coronation. So we can read the second line of verse 50 as saying that God shows steadfast love to David. But David uses the word "anointed" for a particular reason.

5. The book of Matthew begins with these words: "The book of the genealogy of Jesus Christ, the son of David, the son of Abraham."

What are three ways Matthew describes Jesus in this verse?

The word "Christ" means "anointed." What do you think Matthew is saying about Jesus by calling him Jesus *Christ*?

The genealogy in Matthew 1 moves through many generations to get to Jesus. And Jesus could be described as "the son of" any of the men along the way. But Matthew highlights that Jesus is the son of David specifically.

6. Look back at Psalm 18:50. Who do you think is David's offspring, the ultimate king this passage is referring to?

At the end of Psalm 18, David looks forward to his offspring, the coming king who will deliver God's people from their sin. These final verses point to Jesus! But the Psalms don't only point to Jesus; they find their fulfillment in him. That brings us back to verse 41, where David's enemies cried out to God.

7. Read the description of Jesus as he was dying on the cross recorded in Matthew 27:46:

And about the ninth hour Jesus cried out with a loud voice, saying, "Eli, Eli, lema sabachthani?" that is, "My God, my God, why have you forsaken me?"

What did Jesus do at the ninth hour?

_____

_____

Whom did he cry out to?

_____

_____

When Jesus was on the cross, suffering a cruel punishment he didn't deserve, he cried out to God the Father. And God the Father didn't answer. God didn't rescue Jesus from the cross, because Jesus went to the cross to rescue us.

In Psalm 18:41, we find a hard truth about the fate of God's enemies. But it points us to a glorious truth about what Jesus has done to turn God's enemies into his friends. Psalm 18 shows us that God rescued David from his ultimate enemies of sin and death—and through Christ, he rescues us.

8. Have you turned to Christ in faith and experienced God's rescue from sin and death? If so, write a prayer below thanking God for your salvation. If not, write a prayer asking God to show you your need of salvation and help you cry out to him.

_____

_____

_____

_____

HOW TO STUDY THE PSALMS   31

 **Memory Verse**

> In my distress I called upon the LORD;
>   to my God I cried for help.
> From his temple he heard my voice,
>   and my cry to him reached his ears. (Ps. 18:6)

REFLECTION

My grandfather loved the Bible. He preached it for decades as a local church pastor. He meditated on verses he'd memorized as he went to sleep each night. And he read it voraciously.

One Christmas, my family gave him a Bible in a new translation he'd been wanting to read. When we saw him around his birthday in early January, my dad asked if he was enjoying the new Bible. "Oh yes," he said with a big smile, "I read it cover to cover." In just a few weeks, he'd read the entire Bible! There's no telling how many times he read it over the course of his life.

When my grandfather came to the end of his ninety-two years on earth, our family gathered in a hospital room where he was hooked up to machines, semiconscious and barely breathing. But occasionally he mumbled a few words, so my brother leaned in close to listen. "He's reciting a psalm!" my brother said in amazement. Barely clinging to life, he was doing what he'd always done—turning his eyes to Jesus.

I don't think it's a coincidence he was reciting a psalm. He'd memorized verses from all over the Bible, but as Athanasius observed, the Psalms "have a unique place in the Bible because most of Scripture speaks to us, while the Psalms speak for us."[8] The Psalms give us words to pray and sing to God. They show us how to pray when we're angry and hurting. They show us how to sing when we're thankful and rejoicing. They give us words to cling to as we're dying.

But we also find parts of the psalms that we're hesitant to make our own. How can we say with David in Psalm 18 that we're "blameless" (v. 23)? How can we proclaim, "the LORD dealt with me according to my righteousness" (v. 20) when we are so very aware of our sinfulness?

In 2 Corinthians 1:20, Paul explains that "all the promises of God find their Yes in [Jesus]. That is why it is through him that we utter our Amen to God for his glory." We can pray and sing these words along with David, we can utter our Amen, because they are true *in Jesus*. God makes us blameless—in Jesus. God rescues us from our sin—in Jesus. God brings salvation and shows steadfast love to David and his offspring forever—in Jesus. God shows himself to us—in Jesus.

When we turn to the Psalms, we turn our eyes to Jesus.

In those last hours, my grandfather couldn't regale us with a story or carry on a conversation. But for decades upon decades, like David, my grandfather had kept God's word before him. Reciting the word was as natural to him as breathing. So at the end, when all his other faculties were stripped away, those were the two things he did.

After he recited a psalm, as he labored to breathe, we heard him say over and over again, "It's so beautiful!" We don't know for sure, but we think he was seeing glimpses of heaven. And when the breath finally left his lungs, the things of earth having grown strangely dim, his eyes turned to Jesus and looked fully in his wonderful face.

---

8 Christopher Ash, *Teaching Psalms Volume One: From Text to Message* (Christian Focus, 2018), 23.

You and I can't look upon Jesus the way my grandfather can, but we can turn our eyes to see Jesus in the Psalms. We can live in the light of his glory and grace as we make the truths of the Psalms our prayer and song. And if we do, we'll find, as David and my grandfather did, that when we cry out to God—he hears, he answers, and he rescues.

1. Where are your eyes most often turned? Who or what gets most of your attention?

2. How did Psalm 18 turn your eyes to Jesus this week?

Think of a situation in your life that's causing you distress today. Read back through Psalm 18, making it your prayer. Use David's words to help you cry out to God for help.

💙 Memory Verse

> In my distress I called upon the LORD;
>   to my God I cried for help.
> From his temple he heard my voice,
>   and my cry to him reached his ears. (Ps. 18:6)

GROUP DISCUSSION QUESTIONS

Icebreaker: What's your favorite type of music?

Warm-up: Before beginning this study, what was your impression of the Psalms?

1. What did David's opening imagery in Psalm 18 (rock, fortress, shield, stronghold, etc.) convey to you about God's character?

2. Why do you think David describes his enemy as death in verses 4–5 while the superscript identifies David's enemy as Saul?

3. Before looking at other Scripture passages, what did you think David was describing in verses 7–16? How did seeing the connections to other Old Testament stories change your understanding of these verses?

4. Why is it important to consider the structure of a psalm and how its ideas fit together, rather than trying to interpret individual verses on their own?

5. As we study this psalm, how do we understand David's need for rescue as both physical (because of Saul's pursuit) and spiritual (because of sin's condemnation)? How does God rescue David from both types of enemies? In what ways do you need to know God as a refuge, stronghold, and shield today?

6. Why is it significant that David ends Psalm 18 with a reference to his offspring?

7. What was one thing that convicted, encouraged, instructed, or stood out to you this week?

8. How did this psalm help you turn your eyes to Jesus?

What did you see or learn about Jesus?

What do you need to believe as a result?

How should you live differently?

Hymn for the Week

"Turn Your Eyes upon Jesus"

> O soul, are you weary and troubled?
> No light in the darkness you see?
> There's light for a look at the Savior,
> And life more abundant and free!
>
> Turn your eyes upon Jesus,
> Look full in his wonderful face,
> And the things of earth will grow strangely dim,
> In the light of his glory and grace.[9]

---

9   Helen Howarth Lemmel, "Turn Your Eyes upon Jesus," 1922, https://hymnary.org.

Week 2

Turn to God for Wisdom

Psalms 1 and 73

I'm not a runner. But when I moved to Texas, one thing led to another, and I eventually registered for the Austin Marathon. What was I thinking? I didn't know the first thing about running—especially running 26.2 miles! I desperately needed wisdom to know how to train, when to train, what shoes to buy, and so much more. Thankfully I had a few college buddies who were marathon enthusiasts. I reached out to them, and they taught me everything I needed to know. When my big day finally came and I crossed the finish line, I knew I couldn't have done it without their help.

Life is a lot like a marathon. Without proper knowledge and training, it can be brutal! Just as I needed the wisdom of experienced runners, we desperately need God's wisdom to run our spiritual race well. Biblical wisdom is the ability to apply God's principles to particular situations. And don't we all need to know how to do that? We learn how to do this all throughout Scripture but particularly in what is called *Wisdom Literature*. The wisdom books—Job, Ecclesiastes, Song of Songs, Psalms, and Proverbs—are theologically rich yet deeply practical, and their themes are presented in what are called *wisdom psalms*. These poems are a beautiful hybrid of Wisdom Literature and song.

This week we'll explore Psalm 1 and Psalm 73, two wisdom psalms that invite us to drink in God's wisdom as they celebrate the goodness of following his ways. So grab a cup of something wonderful, find a comfy place to work, and let's prepare for a feast in the Scriptures.

⬆ Turn to God in Prayer

Heavenly Father, thank you for revealing your truth in the Psalms. Holy Spirit, please open my eyes as I study, help me understand (Ps. 49:3), and cause me to delight in your word (Ps. 1:2). In Christ's name, amen.

💙 Memory Verse

> Blessed is the man
>   who walks not in the counsel of the wicked,
> nor stands in the way of sinners,
>   nor sits in the seat of scoffers;
> but his delight is in the law of the Lord,
>   and on his law he meditates day and night. (Ps. 1:1–2)

PSALM 1 OBSERVATION AND INTERPRETATION

Psalm 1

The Way of the Righteous and the Wicked

> ¹ Blessed is the man
>   who walks not in the counsel of the wicked,
>   nor stands in the way of sinners,
>   nor sits in the seat of scoffers;

2 but his delight is in the law of the Lord,
    and on his law he meditates day and night.

3 He is like a tree
    planted by streams of water
  that yields its fruit in its season,
    and its leaf does not wither.
  In all that he does, he prospers.
4 The wicked are not so,
    but are like chaff that the wind drives away.

5 Therefore the wicked will not stand in the judgment,
    nor sinners in the congregation of the righteous;
6 for the Lord knows the way of the righteous,
    but the way of the wicked will perish.

Did you know there are only two kinds of people in the world? Many people, when it comes to religion, believe there must be at least three categories: the "super religious," heinous evildoers, and people who are just "good enough" to make it into heaven—if such a place exists.

But here's the thing: the Bible teaches that there's no third option. There are only *two* ways to live, and it calls one foolish and the other wise. Psalm 1, the opening passage of the Psalms, begins with this shocking contrast and urges us to walk in God's ways.

Observation: What Does Psalm 1 Say?

Read Psalm 1 before answering the questions below.

1. Repeated words or ideas in a text help us understand what the author is emphasizing. Read Psalm 1 again, but this time highlight or underline every

instance of the words *righteous* and *wicked* (or their synonyms). Do you notice any other repeated words, phrases, or ideas in the text? Jot them down.

2. What comparison or contrast do you see in this psalm?

3. Using the table below, list everything Psalm 1 teaches about the "righteous" and the "wicked." An example is given to get you started.

The Righteous	The Wicked
He does not walk in the counsel of the wicked. (v. 1)	

4. The imagery of a tree planted by water is not only used in Psalm 1. The prophet Jeremiah also uses it to contrast the cursed man and the blessed man. Read Jeremiah 17:5–8. What similarities do you notice between this passage and Psalm 1? Are there differences?

Interpretation: What Does Psalm 1 Mean?

5. Psalm 1 presents the results of two ways of life. What are they and how does the psalmist convince us one is better than the other?

6. How does the parallelism of verse 2 help us understand what it means to delight in the law of the Lord? Remember, parallelism occurs when two or more lines deal with the same subject.

Many of us have never threshed grain, so we may be unfamiliar with the term "chaff." However, for the original audience, this imagery would have been familiar. In the process of threshing grain, the chaff is the light and useless part that blows away with the wind.

7. What message might the psalmist have been aiming to convey by comparing a righteous person to a tree (v. 3) and a wicked person to chaff (v. 4)?

8. What do you think it means when this Psalm says, "In all that he does, he prospers" (v. 3)? What type of prosperity do you think that refers to?

9. Look back at your answers from today's questions. Write a summary statement that captures the main idea of Psalm 1. *Hint:* Consider the characteristics and the final destinies of the righteous and the wicked.

10. Are you surprised by anything in this psalm? Write any questions you have.

One of the trees in my backyard died last summer. Given the Texas heat, it probably needed more water than our sprinkler system was programmed to give. However, another tree of ours seems to thrive no matter what the weather brings. It's planted at the lowest point of the yard, so every time it rains the water flows down past our patio and drenches its roots. It reminds me of the tree referenced in our psalm today. It's planted in the right place, so its leaves never wither and it survives even the harshest of conditions. I want to be like *that* tree—planted and rooted in the nourishing wisdom of the Lord. Don't you want that too? Today's psalm teaches that we do this by knowing and living in God's word. Let's plant ourselves by his living water so our lives will bear fruit for his glory.

💙 Memory Verse

Blessed is the man
　who walks not in the counsel of the wicked,
nor stands in the way of sinners,
　nor sits in the seat of scoffers;
but his delight is in the law of the Lord,
　and on his law he meditates day and night. (Ps. 1:1–2)

PSALM 1 INTERPRETATION AND APPLICATION

Interpretation: What Does the Whole Bible Say?

Yesterday we learned that the book of Psalms opens with a clear message: there are two ways to live (not three!), and only one of them leads to blessing. Amazingly, this message is woven throughout the whole Bible. From Adam and Eve's fall in Genesis to Christ's triumph in Revelation, we are presented with the drastic difference between the wise and the foolish. Let's spend time today exploring some Old and New Testament passages that help us further understand the message of Psalm 1.

Before you begin, pray and ask God to show you wonderful things in his word. Then read Psalm 1 again before you answer the questions below.

1. According to Psalm 1 there are two ways to live but only one that results in eternal life. Summarize what each of the following verses teaches about the wicked (or foolish) and the righteous.

   Romans 3:10–12

   _____

   _____

   Romans 3:21–26

   _____

   _____

Matthew 5:20

_____

_____

Were you shocked by what you read in Matthew 5:20? According to Jesus, only the righteous will see the face of God. This is bad news for us because none of us is righteous! Christ, the righteous, is the *only* one who can truly sing this psalm. But, thankfully, the story doesn't end there. There's a way we can be *made* righteous.

2. How does 2 Corinthians 5:21 help you understand why Christians can sing Psalm 1 along with Jesus?

_____

_____

_____

_____

If you have placed your faith in Christ, he has made you righteous. And now you can pursue godly living in light of what Christ has done.

Application: How Do I Faithfully Respond?

The Bible's psalms overflow with rich theology as well as practical help for godly living. But knowledge must be put into action. As we close our time in this first wisdom psalm, use the following application questions to consider how you might respond.

3. After the death of Moses, a man named Joshua led the Israelites into the land of promise. But before Joshua assumed command, the Lord provided specific instructions to ensure success. Based on the instructions in Joshua 1:8, what

is the "prosperous life" according to God? As you think about your day, what do you find yourself meditating on? What are some ways you might turn your eyes back to God's word throughout the day?

4. Psalm 1 is honest about the terrible fate of the wicked. How does reading it prompt you to pray for others?

5. What wisdom have you gained by studying Psalm 1? How will you live differently because of what you've learned?

Psalm 1 corrects our thinking. There aren't three ways to live but two. When we turn from sin and trust in Christ, the Holy Spirit comes to dwell inside us so we can wholeheartedly pursue righteous living that accords with Scripture. May we delight in God's word and meditate on it day and night (Ps. 1:2) so we will prosper for his glory and our good.

TURN TO GOD FOR WISDOM 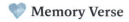 49

💙 Memory Verse

Blessed is the man
   who walks not in the counsel of the wicked,
nor stands in the way of sinners,
   nor sits in the seat of scoffers;
but his delight is in the law of the Lord,
   and on his law he meditates day and night. (Ps. 1:1–2)

PSALM 73 OBSERVATION AND INTERPRETATION

Psalm 73

God Is My Strength and Portion Forever
A Psalm of Asaph.

1 Truly God is good to Israel,
   to those who are pure in heart.
2 But as for me, my feet had almost stumbled,
   my steps had nearly slipped.
3 For I was envious of the arrogant
   when I saw the prosperity of the wicked.

4 For they have no pangs until death;
   their bodies are fat and sleek.
5 They are not in trouble as others are;
   they are not stricken like the rest of mankind.
6 Therefore pride is their necklace;
   violence covers them as a garment.
7 Their eyes swell out through fatness;
   their hearts overflow with follies.
8 They scoff and speak with malice;
   loftily they threaten oppression.

50 TURN TO GOD FOR WISDOM

9 They set their mouths against the heavens,
    and their tongue struts through the earth.
10 Therefore his people turn back to them,
    and find no fault in them.
11 And they say, "How can God know?
    Is there knowledge in the Most High?"
12 Behold, these are the wicked;
    always at ease, they increase in riches.
13 All in vain have I kept my heart clean
    and washed my hands in innocence.
14 For all the day long I have been stricken
    and rebuked every morning.
15 If I had said, "I will speak thus,"
    I would have betrayed the generation of your children.

16 But when I thought how to understand this,
    it seemed to me a wearisome task,
17 until I went into the sanctuary of God;
    then I discerned their end.

18 Truly you set them in slippery places;
    you make them fall to ruin.
19 How they are destroyed in a moment,
    swept away utterly by terrors!
20 Like a dream when one awakes,
    O Lord, when you rouse yourself, you despise them as phantoms.
21 When my soul was embittered,
    when I was pricked in heart,
22 I was brutish and ignorant;
    I was like a beast toward you.

23 Nevertheless, I am continually with you;
    you hold my right hand.

^{24} You guide me with your counsel,
  and afterward you will receive me to glory.
^{25} Whom have I in heaven but you?
  And there is nothing on earth that I desire besides you.
^{26} My flesh and my heart may fail,
  but God is the strength of my heart and my portion forever.

^{27} For behold, those who are far from you shall perish;
  you put an end to everyone who is unfaithful to you.
^{28} But for me it is good to be near God;
  I have made the Lord GOD my refuge,
  that I may tell of all your works.

Observation: What Does Psalm 73 Say?

Psalm 1 reminded us that wisdom is found by delighting in God's word. Today and tomorrow we will study Psalm 73, a wisdom psalm that deals with another common topic found throughout the Bible. Interestingly, although it was written long ago, it answers a question still being asked today: How should we respond to injustice?

As we did on day 1, we'll observe the text and use our observations to discern the author's main message. Remember to pray, asking God to give you wisdom as you read and study. Then read Psalm 73 a few times. As you read, mark any repeated words, phrases, and ideas you notice.

1. Read the superscription. Who wrote this psalm? What do you learn about him in 1 Chronicles 15:16–17?

In this psalm, Asaph uses two literary devices to make his point: simile and metaphor. A *simile* uses "like" or "as" to compare two things. For example, in verse 22 Asaph says he was "like a beast" before God. A *metaphor*, on the other hand, describes something by saying it *is* something else. When Asaph calls "pride" a "necklace" in verse 6, he's using a metaphor. Pride is not actually a piece of jewelry that hangs around your neck!

2. Why did Asaph nearly stumble (v. 3)?

3. List out Asaph's description of the wicked in verses 1–12.

4. How does Asaph describe his feelings in each of the following parts of the psalm? Notice how his attitude changes.

Verses 1–3

Verses 13–14

Verses 15–22

Verses 23–28

I don't know about you, but I talk to myself all the time. Although I chuckle a bit when I catch someone else doing this, it's actually a helpful habit. As I verbalize my thoughts and feelings, my talking often turns to prayer. In prayer, I am reminded that by God's Spirit I can take every thought captive to obey Christ, meaning I can adjust my sinful thinking by speaking gospel truths to myself. This is what changes us! And as we learn to do this more and more, we will become the kind of people who know God's word and walk in his ways.

In Psalm 73 Asaph describes the shift that took place in his thinking as he contemplated God's truths (perhaps out loud). Now that we have taken a look at Asaph's progression of thoughts, let's think about the psalm's meaning.

Interpretation: What Does Psalm 73 Mean?

5. In the first half of Psalm 73 Asaph explains he had been envious of the wicked, but in verses 15–17 he discusses a shift in perspective. Why do you think

entering the sanctuary and contemplating the fate of the wicked helped him think differently?

6. Based on the conclusion Asaph draws in verses 25–28, what is the main message of this psalm? Try to summarize it in one or two short sentences.

7. What surprised or caught your attention as you read this psalm today? List any questions you have.

When my husband and I were building our current home, I spent a lot of time seeking inspiration from dream kitchen websites, but our limited budget offered no allowance for the expensive upgrades featured on the internet. Our selections could not compare to the fancy, top-of-the-line products with all the bells and whistles so my search for inspiration ended in envy and discontentment. In today's psalm, Asaph compares his life to others' and becomes envious to the point of nearly stumbling away from God. But he reorients his thinking by meditating on God's goodness. Let's pray with Asaph that we would desire nothing more than we desire God. May the Lord be our portion forever (Ps. 73:25-26).

Memory Verse

> Blessed is the man
>   who walks not in the counsel of the wicked,
> nor stands in the way of sinners,
>   nor sits in the seat of scoffers;
> but his delight is in the law of the LORD,
>   and on his law he meditates day and night. (Ps. 1:1-2)

PSALM 73 INTERPRETATION AND APPLICATION

Interpretation: What Does the Whole Bible Say?

The Psalms are unique in that they teach biblical truths while addressing the various emotions we experience in life. As we have seen, the poetic devices in Psalm 73 help us identify with Asaph's initial discouragement over apparent injustices and his later resolution to put his hope in God. This is one of the ways psalms teach wisdom! They show us how to handle our feelings.

Today we will consider some New Testament passages that deepen our understanding of Asaph's message. Before you answer the questions below, read Psalm 73 again and pray for God's help as you study.

1. In the New Testament, Jesus tells a story to illustrate the fate of the wicked. Read Luke 16:19–31 and answer the following questions.

What happens to Lazarus when he dies? What happens to the rich man when he dies?

We know being rich is not sinful. Instead, it's the *love* of money—loving it and desiring it more than we love and desire God—that corrupts (1 Tim. 6:10). If the rich man is not condemned simply for having money, why does he end up in Hades?

How might Jesus's story of Lazarus and the rich man help you understand the main point of Psalm 73?

Peter, one of Jesus's disciples, wrote a letter in the early first century to encourage Christians facing persecution under the Roman emperor, Nero. Much like Psalm 73, this letter reorients our thinking and reminds us to keep living for God. Read 1 Peter 1:3–9 and then consider the following questions.

2. Though some Christians may be wealthy, God has not promised us riches on earth. Based on 1 Peter 1:3–9, what *has* God promised his people?

3. Asaph says the wicked "are always at ease" (Ps. 73:12) but the righteous have been "stricken" (vv. 5, 14) and "rebuked every morning" (v. 14). How does 1 Peter 1:3–9 shed light on this apparent injustice?

In both these passages, Luke 16:19–31 and 1 Peter 1:3–9, suffering is not the end of the story. This is another common theme throughout the wisdom psalms: Christians will have trouble, but God will not forsake us. Asaph envied the wicked when he contemplated their comforts, but his shift in thinking came when he realized their fate. They will perish, but God's people will be saved.

Application: How Do I Faithfully Respond?

Now it's time to think about how to apply what we have learned to our own lives. Ask the Lord for his help and use the questions below as a guide.

4. In verse 13 Asaph wonders if it is worth it to follow God. Have you ever felt this way? How does Psalm 73 help you think differently about the struggles of life?

5. Psalm 73 reminds us that material possessions cannot compare to knowing God. How have you been tempted to cherish *things* more than your relationship with the Lord?

6. What wisdom have you gleaned by studying Psalm 73?

During my marathon training, one of my running friends said, "On race day, just keep putting one foot in front of the other, and eventually you'll cross the finish line." She was so right. As I ran those last few miles, the promise of a cold drink and a soft oatmeal cookie was just the motivation I needed to finish. According to Scripture, God has prepared a much more satisfying prize for us. Those who walk with God will cross the finish line to receive eternal life. And yes, it will be worth it.

🩵 Memory Verse

> Blessed is the man
>   who walks not in the counsel of the wicked,
> nor stands in the way of sinners,
>   nor sits in the seat of scoffers;
> but his delight is in the law of the LORD,
>   and on his law he meditates day and night. (Ps. 1:1–2)

REFLECTION

I used to love telling people about how busy I was. I would half-heartedly complain about this commitment and that deadline, all the while knowing I secretly loved talking about all the things I was doing. In some ways it made me feel important to humbly brag about everything I needed to get done in a day, and I would often say things like "I don't have time for that!" But over the years I have learned that *man does what man most wants to do*. I always make time for the things most important to me like eating healthy meals, brushing and flossing my teeth, and working out.

I stopped bragging about my busyness because I realized we all get the same twenty-four hours in a day. We can choose to spend those hours wisely or unwisely, and whether we admit it or not, we make time for the things most important to us. The wisdom psalms teach Christians that what should be most important to us is seeking God through his word so we can live skillfully in the time we've been given.

Wisdom psalms teach us to live skillfully according to God's truths in three significant ways. First, they are deeply practical because they teach us to apply God's truths to the situations we face. Consider, for example, Psalm 112:7, which tells us not to be afraid of bad news but instead to trust in the Lord. This is exactly what we need to remember before we read the latest headlines. Another example is Psalm 119:147, which suggests we should "rise before dawn" to "cry for help." The psalmist knew that we need to ask for help *before* the challenges come.

Second, wisdom psalms train us in ethical behavior that trades sin and wickedness for obedience and holiness. We see this in Psalm 49:5–9, which condemns the practice of cheating for financial gain and again in Psalm 37:14–15, which warns against mistreatment of the poor.

Finally, wisdom psalms are theologically rich. They teach us about God and call us to serve him alone. From Psalm 19 we learn,

> The heavens declare the glory of God,
>   and the sky above proclaims his handiwork. (v. 1)

And Psalm 37 reminds us to trust God's sovereignty in times of suffering.

> The salvation of the righteous is from the LORD;
>   he is their stronghold in the time of trouble.
> The LORD helps them and delivers them;
>   he delivers them from the wicked and saves them,
>   because they take refuge in him. (vv. 39–40)

As we meditate on wisdom psalms we soon realize none of us is perfectly wise. Though we might take hold of every tool God provides for growth, we will never achieve perfection in this lifetime. But Christ is not like us. He is the embodiment of wisdom and has lived the perfectly wise life in our place. As we rest in what he has accomplished on our behalf, we can confidently pursue growth in godliness.

How should we respond to the wisdom psalms? How can we become wise women? We have learned the wise woman avoids the counsel of the wicked. Instead, she meditates day and night on God's word. She is not envious of the temporary comforts afforded to those who ignore God. She knows she has everything because she has God. Therefore, she is not tempted to value earthly things more than the Lord. God is the strength of her heart and her portion forever.

Friend, I pray that the wisdom psalms would encourage you to choose God's ways, knowing we have everything we need to live godly lives (2 Pet. 1:3). Sing these truths to yourself today as you meditate on his wisdom!

1. How might reading, praying, and singing wisdom psalms encourage you in every season of life?

2. How did Psalm 1 and Psalm 73 turn your eyes to Jesus this week?

💙 Memory Verse

> Blessed is the man
> who walks not in the counsel of the wicked,
> nor stands in the way of sinners,
> nor sits in the seat of scoffers;
> but his delight is in the law of the Lord,
> and on his law he meditates day and night. (Ps. 1:1–2)

GROUP DISCUSSION QUESTIONS

Icebreaker: If you could immediately become an expert in a particular subject, what would it be?

Warm-up: What's a piece of advice or wisdom someone shared with you that you often share with others?

1. The author of Psalm 1 compares the righteous one to a tree and the wicked one to chaff. How do these comparisons help you understand the life God blesses?

2. Why is it important to read and meditate on God's word?

3. How do wisdom psalms help us think rightly about the prosperity of the wicked?

4. When you are seeking wisdom, where do you most often turn? To a person? Podcast? Book? What would it look like for you to turn to the Psalms for wisdom?

5. Asaph's negative perspective shifted after he spent time with God's people. What does this teach about the importance of the local church?

6. Meditating on God's nature and his promises helped Asaph. What aspects of God's character are most significant to you in times of doubt or struggle?

7. What was one thing that convicted, encouraged, instructed, or stood out to you this week?

8. How did these psalms help you turn your eyes to Jesus?

What did you see or learn about Jesus?

What do you need to believe as a result?

How should you live differently?

♪ Hymn for the Week

"Be Thou My Vision"

Be Thou my vision, O Lord of my heart;
Naught be all else to me, save that Thou art;
Thou my best thought, by day or by night,
Waking or sleeping, Thy presence my light.[1]

Additional Wisdom Psalms for Further Study

Psalms 19, 36, 37, 49, 50, 78, 112, 119, 127, and 133

We've listed general questions in an appendix that you can use while studying these psalms.

---

1   Eleanor H. Hull, "Be Thou My Vision," trans. Mary E. Byrne, 1927, https://hymnary.org.

Week 3

Turn to God with Thanksgiving

Psalms 34 and 107

Jesus once healed ten people with leprosy and only *one* returned to say thanks. Leprosy was a horrible, highly contagious skin disease that rendered its victims too dangerous for participation in society. So naturally we're shocked when we read that nine of the men failed to show proper gratitude for their miraculous healing. But if I'm honest, I'm more like the nine than the one. It isn't that I necessarily forget to thank God for his blessings. The deeper issue is that I have a general tendency to grumble and complain about my circumstances instead of being grateful for all God has done for me. Sometimes I need to be reminded that God is good and deserves my gratitude—regardless of what's happening in my life.

This week we turn to thanksgiving psalms, which show us that God, our refuge and deliverer, is the right recipient of our thanks. In these psalms the authors praise God for answered prayer and invite the reader to do the same. A heart of thankfulness is important because it helps us develop humility, deepens our faith, and cultivates contentment. This week we'll see that God has done more than enough to prove he is worthy of our gratitude.

Turn to God in Prayer

Thank you, God, for your steadfast love and faithfulness (Ps. 107:1). As I study, help me to taste and see that you are good (Ps. 34:8). Holy Spirit, please fill my heart with gratitude for all that Christ has done. In Jesus's name, amen.

Memory Verse

> I will bless the LORD at all times;
>   his praise shall continually be in my mouth. (Ps. 34:1)

PSALM 34 OBSERVATION AND INTERPRETATION

Psalm 34

Taste and See That the LORD Is Good
Of David, when he changed his behavior before Abimelech, so that he drove him out, and he went away.

> 1 I will bless the LORD at all times;
>   his praise shall continually be in my mouth.
> 2 My soul makes its boast in the LORD;
>   let the humble hear and be glad.
> 3 Oh, magnify the LORD with me,
>   and let us exalt his name together!
>
> 4 I sought the LORD, and he answered me
>   and delivered me from all my fears.

5   Those who look to him are radiant,
        and their faces shall never be ashamed.
6   This poor man cried, and the LORD heard him
        and saved him out of all his troubles.
7   The angel of the LORD encamps
        around those who fear him, and delivers them.

8   Oh, taste and see that the LORD is good!
        Blessed is the man who takes refuge in him!
9   Oh, fear the LORD, you his saints,
        for those who fear him have no lack!
10 The young lions suffer want and hunger;
        but those who seek the LORD lack no good thing.

11 Come, O children, listen to me;
        I will teach you the fear of the LORD.
12 What man is there who desires life
        and loves many days, that he may see good?
13 Keep your tongue from evil
        and your lips from speaking deceit.
14 Turn away from evil and do good;
        seek peace and pursue it.

15 The eyes of the LORD are toward the righteous
        and his ears toward their cry.
16 The face of the LORD is against those who do evil,
        to cut off the memory of them from the earth.
17 When the righteous cry for help, the LORD hears
        and delivers them out of all their troubles.
18 The LORD is near to the brokenhearted
        and saves the crushed in spirit.

19 Many are the afflictions of the righteous,
    but the LORD delivers him out of them all.
20 He keeps all his bones;
    not one of them is broken.
21 Affliction will slay the wicked,
    and those who hate the righteous will be condemned.
22 The LORD redeems the life of his servants;
    none of those who take refuge in him will be condemned.

Observation: What Does Psalm 34 Say?

Have you ever witnessed or experienced a near miss while driving? It makes your heart skip a beat, and when the dust settles you realize just how close you were to disaster.

According to its superscription, Psalm 34 was written by King David, a man who knew what it was like to narrowly escape grave danger. While on the run from King Saul, David fled to the city of Gath but was quickly recognized by their king. Fearing for his life, he pretended to be a madman. The plan worked, and the king drove him out of town. In Psalm 34 David expressed his gratitude for God's deliverance.

Read Psalm 34 and, as you read, mark the following key words and their synonyms: *good*, *delivers*, *righteous*, *wicked*. Then answer the following questions.

1. David opens this psalm by expressing his desire to worship God. In verses 1–3, how does he describe his intentions? What does he invite his listener to do?

TURN TO GOD WITH THANKSGIVING · 71

2. According to verses 4–7, what did David do when he faced danger in Abimelech's presence? How did God respond?

3. Read verses 8–10 and list the blessings that come to those who fear the Lord.

4. In verses 15–22, what words and phrases describe God's actions toward the righteous?

Now that we've made some initial observations, let's take a closer look at the figurative language and poetic structure David uses so we can better understand this psalm.

Interpretation: What Does Psalm 34 Mean?

As we learned in week 1, Hebrew poetry often uses parallelism to convey ideas. There are three main forms of parallelism that appear in Psalms: synonymous, antithetical, and synthetic. *Synonymous parallelism* uses a second line to bring clarity to the first and often highlights some aspect of the author's emphasis. We find a few examples of this in Psalm 34. Take a look at verses 1–3 again.

5. How does the second line of each of these verses highlight or bring clarity to what is described in the first line? What is being emphasized?

> I will bless the LORD at all times;
>> his praise shall continually be in my mouth. (v. 1)

> Oh, magnify the LORD with me,
>> And let us exalt his name together! (v. 3)

6. In the following chart, notice how David uses repeated words and ideas to tie his experience to what God's people, in general, experience.[1]

---

1 James M. Hamilton Jr., *Psalms Volume I: Evangelical Biblical Theology Commentary* (Lexham Academic, 2021), 379.

David's Experience	The Experience of God's People
"I <u>sought the LORD</u>, and he answered me and delivered me from all my fears." (v. 4)	"The young lions suffer want and hunger; but those who <u>seek the LORD</u> lack no good thing." (v. 10)
"This poor man <u>cried</u>, and the LORD heard him / and <u>saved him</u> out of all his troubles." (v. 6)	"When the righteous <u>cry</u> for help, the LORD hears / and <u>delivers them</u> out of all their troubles." (v. 17)

What connection is David drawing with these comparisons?

7. In the last eight verses of the psalm (vv. 15–22) David contrasts the righteous and the wicked to highlight God's faithfulness to his people. Notice that both the righteous (v. 19) and the wicked (v. 21) experience afflictions. How does God use afflictions in the life of the righteous one? And how does he use affliction in the life of the wicked one?

At this point, you might be wondering why Psalm 34 is known as a psalm of thanksgiving. Although David never actually uses the phrase "give thanks," through this psalm he shows us what it looks like to be thankful. He wants to spread the news, "God is good! God is faithful! He delivered me, and he will deliver you too!" God is worthy of our thanks and praise.

💙 Memory Verse

> I will bless the LORD at all times;
> his praise shall continually be in my mouth. (Ps. 34:1)

PSALM 34 INTERPRETATION AND APPLICATION

Interpretation: What Does the Whole Bible Say?

When my son was a toddler, he needed my help all the time. Not anymore! He's a fairly self-sufficient teenager now, so it warms my heart on the rare occasions when I hear him cry out for help. A momma loves to come to her child's rescue.

Throughout the Scriptures, God describes himself as a loving Father who desires to rescue his children from their trouble. We know God rescued David from a dangerous situation in Gath, but David isn't the only one with this kind of testimony. Today we will look at a few other places in Scripture that reiterate God's goodness and the thankfulness he deserves. Begin your study time with prayer, asking God to show you wonderful things in his word.

1. Read Ephesians 5:15–21. In this passage, Paul links thanksgiving to corporate singing. How does this passage help you understand David's invitation in Psalm 34:1–3? Why does he want others to join him in praise?

_____

_____

2. The Israelites spent years as slaves in Egypt, but when they cried out to God, he came to their rescue. Read Exodus 2:23–25 and 14:30–15:18, and answer the following questions:

Why did the people cry out to God?

How did God respond?

Compare Exodus 15:1–18 and Psalm 34. What similarities do you notice between Moses's response to deliverance from Egypt and David's response to deliverance from the danger in Gath?

3. Peter quotes Psalm 34:12–16 in 1 Peter 3:8–13. Compare these two passages and explain how Peter uses Psalm 34 to make his point.

The Israelites suffered in Egypt for 430 years before God brought them out of the land (Ex. 12:40). To ensure they would never forget their dramatic rescue, God instituted the Passover feast during which the people were to sacrifice a lamb by killing it without breaking its bones (Ex. 12:43–51).

Many years later, John introduces Jesus as "the Lamb of God" (John 1:29) and writes in his account of Christ's crucifixion, "For these things took place that the Scripture might be fulfilled: 'Not one of his bones will be broken'" (John 19:36). Jesus was the Passover lamb who died for our sins, but three days later God raised him from the dead.

4. How do Jesus's death and resurrection help you understand what David means in Psalm 34:19–22 when he explains God's deliverance of the righteous ones?

5. David's main message in Psalm 34 is an exhortation—we should bless the Lord who delivers the righteous from all their troubles. Consider Matthew 10:28 and Romans 5:8–11. What is man's greatest problem, and how has God solved it?

King David wrote Psalm 34 to express thanks to God who sustained him through many afflictions, but this psalm also applies to Christ's crucifixion (John 19:31–37). Jesus was afflicted (Ps. 34:19) and killed, but his bones were never broken. Jesus is the Passover lamb who died in our place and rose from the grave, solving our greatest problem.

Application: How Do I Faithfully Respond?

Use the following questions to help you consider how you might respond to this beautiful psalm.

6. In Psalm 34, David expresses thankfulness for God's deliverance. In what ways have you experienced God's deliverance? What words or phrases of this psalm encourage you to give thanks for your own deliverance?

7. How might you "taste" and "see" more of God? Write two or three things you can do over the next few weeks to learn more about God's goodness.

Why would a writer tell a story using poetry instead of prose? One benefit of poetic expression is that it moves beyond the details of a story to an author's *feelings* about it, which can often aid the reader in responding properly to the circumstances of life. The figurative language and imagery in Psalm 34 are meant to evoke feelings of gratitude so we might join all who say, "Oh, magnify the Lord with me, and let us exalt his name together!" (v. 3).

💙 Memory Verse for the Week

> I will bless the Lord at all times;
>   his praise shall continually be in my mouth. (Ps. 34:1)

PSALM 107 OBSERVATION AND INTERPRETATION

Psalm 107

Let the Redeemed of the Lord Say So

¹ Oh give thanks to the Lord, for he is good,
  for his steadfast love endures forever!
² Let the redeemed of the Lord say so,
  whom he has redeemed from trouble
³ and gathered in from the lands,
  from the east and from the west,
  from the north and from the south.

⁴ Some wandered in desert wastes,
  finding no way to a city to dwell in;
⁵ hungry and thirsty,
  their soul fainted within them.
⁶ Then they cried to the Lord in their trouble,
  and he delivered them from their distress.
⁷ He led them by a straight way
  till they reached a city to dwell in.

8 Let them thank the Lord for his steadfast love,
   for his wondrous works to the children of man!
9 For he satisfies the longing soul,
   and the hungry soul he fills with good things.

10 Some sat in darkness and in the shadow of death,
   prisoners in affliction and in irons,
11 for they had rebelled against the words of God,
   and spurned the counsel of the Most High.
12 So he bowed their hearts down with hard labor;
   they fell down, with none to help.
13 Then they cried to the Lord in their trouble,
   and he delivered them from their distress.
14 He brought them out of darkness and the shadow of death,
   and burst their bonds apart.
15 Let them thank the Lord for his steadfast love,
   for his wondrous works to the children of man!
16 For he shatters the doors of bronze
   and cuts in two the bars of iron.

17 Some were fools through their sinful ways,
   and because of their iniquities suffered affliction;
18 they loathed any kind of food,
   and they drew near to the gates of death.
19 Then they cried to the Lord in their trouble,
   and he delivered them from their distress.
20 He sent out his word and healed them,
   and delivered them from their destruction.
21 Let them thank the Lord for his steadfast love,
   for his wondrous works to the children of man!
22 And let them offer sacrifices of thanksgiving,
   and tell of his deeds in songs of joy!

23 Some went down to the sea in ships,
   doing business on the great waters;
24 they saw the deeds of the LORD,
   his wondrous works in the deep.
25 For he commanded and raised the stormy wind,
   which lifted up the waves of the sea.
26 They mounted up to heaven; they went down to the depths;
   their courage melted away in their evil plight;
27 they reeled and staggered like drunken men
   and were at their wits' end.
28 Then they cried to the LORD in their trouble,
   and he delivered them from their distress.
29 He made the storm be still,
   and the waves of the sea were hushed.
30 Then they were glad that the waters were quiet,
   and he brought them to their desired haven.
31 Let them thank the LORD for his steadfast love,
   for his wondrous works to the children of man!
32 Let them extol him in the congregation of the people,
   and praise him in the assembly of the elders.

33 He turns rivers into a desert,
   springs of water into thirsty ground,
34 a fruitful land into a salty waste,
   because of the evil of its inhabitants.
35 He turns a desert into pools of water,
   a parched land into springs of water.
36 And there he lets the hungry dwell,
   and they establish a city to live in;
37 they sow fields and plant vineyards
   and get a fruitful yield.
38 By his blessing they multiply greatly,
   and he does not let their livestock diminish.

39 When they are diminished and brought low
  through oppression, evil, and sorrow,
40 he pours contempt on princes
  and makes them wander in trackless wastes;
41 but he raises up the needy out of affliction
  and makes their families like flocks.
42 The upright see it and are glad,
  and all wickedness shuts its mouth.

43 Whoever is wise, let him attend to these things;
  let them consider the steadfast love of the LORD.

Today we will look at another thanksgiving psalm, Psalm 107. While Psalm 34 focused on a personal example from the author's life, this psalm provides four situations in which people cry out to God in their distress. As a result, not only will we likely identify with some of the dilemmas presented in this psalm but we will also understand God's goodness.

Save us, O Lord our God,
  and gather us from among the nations,
that we may give thanks to your holy name
  and glory in your praise. (Ps. 106:47)

This prayer provides the backdrop for Psalm 107, our next thanksgiving psalm. Keep this petition in mind as you read and study today. Open your time with a prayer of your own, asking God to give you wisdom and insight.

Observation: What Does Psalm 107 Say?

Read Psalm 107 two or three times. As you read, mark the following repeated phrases and key words you find such as *steadfast love*, *he delivered them*, and *city to dwell/live in*.

82 TURN TO GOD WITH THANKSGIVING

1. What sentences are repeated throughout this psalm?

2. This psalm includes four examples of God's response to people who cry out to him in their distress. This may describe four different groups of people or it may simply be four ways of describing the same community of sufferers. In each of the sections listed below, what kind of distress are the people facing and how does God respond? The first section is completed for you as an example.

vv. 4–9

These people wandered in desert wastes and had no city in which to dwell. They were hungry and thirsty, but when they cried out to God he led them to a city where they could dwell, and he filled their hungry souls.

vv. 10–16

vv. 17–22

vv. 23–32

3. Sometimes a biblical author includes information at the beginning and at the end of a passage to convey the main point. Write the first and last verses of this psalm. What do these verses have in common?

Interpretation: What Does Psalm 107 Mean?

To understand this psalm, we must understand Israel's exile. In the early sixth century BC the Davidic kingdom existed as a northern region called Israel and a southern region called Judah. Over the years, God's people continually turned to idols. Although God sent many prophets to warn them of coming judgment, they failed to repent. This led to devastating results. In 722 BC the northern kingdom was pillaged by the Assyrians (2 Kings 18:11–12) and in 587 BC the southern kingdom was destroyed by the Babylonians (25:20–21). The beautiful temple was burned, and most of the Israelites were taken as exiles (2 Chronicles 36). Through foreign nations, God poured out his judgment on his people and scattered them away from their land (Deut. 29:27–28). He promised that their exile would be long (Jer. 29:28) but that he would one day gather them back to their place (Jer. 29:14). In the exile, God judged his people, but he never abandoned them. Just as he promised, he came to their rescue by gathering them back to himself (Ezra 1–2).

Keep the context of Israel's exile in mind as you answer the following interpretation questions.

4. The author of Psalm 107 begins and ends with a call to consider God's steadfast love (see v. 1 and v. 43). How is he using the body of the psalm (vv. 4–42)? What does the structure of the psalm emphasize?

5. Read Deuteronomy 30:1–3. How does this passage help you understand Psalm 107?

6. How does the psalmist's use of imagery display the desperation of the ones in distress? Give examples.

7. In question 2, you considered four descriptions of exile. Use what you learned in answering that question to help you answer the following questions.

In what ways are the four descriptions similar? How are they different?

What do the four descriptions of God's response teach you about his character?

David exhorts the reader four times in this psalm, "Let them thank the LORD for his steadfast love, / for his wondrous works to the children of man!" (Ps. 107:8, 15, 21, 31). Isn't it amazing that God would demonstrate his love by responding to his people? He is worthy of our gratitude.

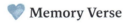 **Memory Verse**

> I will bless the LORD at all times;
> his praise shall continually be in my mouth. (Ps. 34:1)

PSALM 107 INTERPRETATION AND APPLICATION

Interpretation: What Does the Whole Bible Say?

Yesterday we took a close look at Psalm 107 and learned how the psalmist used a four-part structure to make his point. But our work is not quite done. Today we will look at passages from the rest of the Bible to help us develop a more robust understanding of Psalm 107's message. Open your study time by asking God to show you his goodness from the pages of Scripture.

1. Some of the imagery used in Psalm 107 is also used in the New Testament to describe people who need God's help. Explain how each of the following comparisons deepens your understanding of the distress mentioned in Psalm 107.

   Compare Psalm 107:4–9 with John 6:35. How does God help the ones who hunger?

   Compare Psalm 107:10–16 with Colossians 1:13–14. How does God help those in darkness?

   Compare Psalm 107:17–22 with Titus 3:3–7. How does God help the foolish?

   Compare Psalm 107:23–32 with Mark 4:35–41. How does God help those in stormy seas?

2. The apostle Paul experienced much affliction in his ministry of spreading the gospel and planting churches. Read 2 Corinthians 1:3–11, his encouraging words to the Corinthian church, and answer the following questions.

What does Paul say we share with Christ?

Whom does God deliver, and what kind of deliverance does he provide?

How does this passage help you understand Psalm 107?

3. Psalm 107:41 says, "He raises up the needy out of affliction." This points forward to an even greater kind of "raising up." What will Jesus do for those who believe in him (John 6:40)?

Romans 10:13 teaches that everyone who calls on the Lord will be saved. On judgment day, God will raise us up to eternal life just as he resurrected Jesus from the grave. Have you called on the Lord for salvation? If you have, thank God for his steadfast love shown to you in Christ.

Application: How Do I Faithfully Respond?

Although we know how to thank other people, it might be hard to know how to express thankfulness to God. It might even feel awkward or uncomfortable. But studying psalms of thanksgiving helps us develop language to express our gratitude in prayer and praise. Use the following questions to consider how you might respond to God's amazing, never-ending love.

4. Think about a time when you faced trouble. How did you respond? In our study of thanksgiving psalms, what new insights have you gained about crying out to God when you need help?

5. In 2 Corinthians, Paul explains he asked God to take away an affliction that plagued him. Instead of removing the problem, God did something else. Read 2 Corinthians 12:7–10. Can you think of a time when you asked God to deliver you from something difficult but your circumstances never changed? How does Psalm 107 encourage us to think about situations like that?

6. If you are a Christian, write a prayer or poem thanking God for hearing your cry for forgiveness and delivering you from darkness. If you're not, write a

prayer asking God to help you understand your need for salvation and to give you the gift of faith in Christ.

_____

_____

_____

First Chronicles 16 explains that King David instituted practices of worship and appointed certain men to lead the people in daily giving thanks to God. Thankfulness was important to them, and it should be important to us. Thankfulness combats discontentment, it keeps us humble, and it deepens our affection for God. "Oh give thanks to the Lord, for he is good; / for his steadfast love endures forever!" (1 Chron. 16:34).

💙 Memory Verse

> I will bless the Lord at all times;
>   his praise shall continually be in my mouth. (Ps. 34:1)

REFLECTION

I've been afraid of water since the day I nearly drowned. My mom took me to a pool party and since I had never learned to swim, I was told to stay on a raft. Unfortunately, not only did I not know how to swim, apparently I also had no idea how to stay on a raft. At some point during the party, I went under. I remember trying to scream for help, but water filled my mouth so fast. I'm not sure how long it took, but one of the party-goers saved me. He reached in, scooped me up, and gently placed me on dry land.

I'm sure I didn't thank the man enough, but now that I'm an adult with children of my own, gratitude fills my heart when I think about how differently that day could have ended. Oftentimes we fail to recognize the danger we're in until after we have been rescued.

Perhaps this is why many thanksgiving psalms recount God's past acts of deliverance. When we reflect on the way God has demonstrated his love for us, we want to give him thanks. He has proven himself to be loving, kind, and faithful, so we should respond with gratitude.

This doesn't mean, however, that God always removes trials and suffering from our lives. Sometimes he has a greater vision for the kind of rescue we need. Nonetheless, we can pray in confidence, knowing that God will deliver his people because he has already saved us from our greatest form of trouble. Our greatest trouble is that we are sinners (Rom. 3:23) who deserve God's wrath (6:23). But God so loved us that he sent his son, Jesus, to live the perfect life we fail to live and to die the death we all deserve so all who call on the name of Christ will be saved (10:13). God promises that when we cry out to him, confessing our sin, he will come to our rescue and save us. In this world we may have trouble, but our ultimate rescue is secure in Christ. He will deliver us. He already has.

After my near-drowning, I stayed away from water and allowed fear to dictate many of my decisions. I wish I could tell you God has delivered me from it, but he hasn't. I went on to take adult swim lessons and even completed a few open-water triathlons, but I'm still timid at the beach or when standing near the deep end of a pool. The Lord has not removed my *every* fear—I'm still a little afraid of the water and many other things—but thankfully, he has removed my *greatest* fear.

Through his life, death, and resurrection, Christ has delivered us from the worst kind of trouble. So with thankfulness we can say like the apostle Paul, "The Lord will rescue me from every evil deed and bring me safely into his heavenly kingdom. To him be the glory forever and ever. Amen" (2 Tim. 4:18).

1. When is it hard for you to be thankful?

2. How did Psalms 34 and Psalm 107 turn your eyes to Jesus this week?

💙 Memory Verse

> I will bless the Lord at all times;
> his praise shall continually be in my mouth. (Ps. 34:1)

GROUP DISCUSSION QUESTIONS

Icebreaker: What is your favorite holiday side dish and why?

Warm-up: What are you thankful for today?

1. Why is it important to give God thanks? How did the figurative language and imagery in this week's psalms help you understand this?

2. Both Psalm 34 and Psalm 107 begin with an invitation to join the psalmist in praise. What does this convey about the purpose of corporate worship? When you sing at church, how do you encourage others to praise God with you?

3. What are the benefits of recounting God's past faithfulness? How does this cultivate thankfulness?

4. If you're honest, do you spend more time thanking God for what he has done for you or asking him to do more? Consider the acronym ACTS (Adoration, Confession, Thanksgiving, Supplication) as a pattern for daily prayer. How might you use this method to incorporate thanksgiving into your regular prayer times?

5. In Psalm 34:19–21, we learned that both the righteous and the wicked experience afflictions, but God provides deliverance for the righteous. How might this help you as you face difficulties in life? What hope do you find in this psalm?

6. The author of Psalm 107 repeatedly tells the reader to "thank the LORD for his steadfast love." How do you know that God loves you? How has he demonstrated his love?

7. What was one thing that convicted, encouraged, instructed, or stood out to you this week?

8. How did these psalms help you turn your eyes to Jesus?

What did you see or learn about Jesus?

_____

_____

What do you need to believe as a result?

_____

_____

How should you live differently?

_____

_____

♪ Hymn for the Week

"Great Is Thy Faithfulness"

Great is Thy faithfulness, O God my Father;
There is no shadow of turning with Thee;
Thou changest not, Thy compassions, they fail not;
As Thou hast been, Thou forever will be.

Great is Thy faithfulness!
Great is Thy faithfulness!
Morning by morning new mercies I see;
All I have needed Thy hand hath provided:
Great is Thy faithfulness, Lord, unto me![2]

---

2 Thomas O. Chisholm, "Great Is Thy Faithfulness," 1923, https://hymnary.org.

Additional Thanksgiving Psalms for Further Study

Psalms 21, 30, 65, 75, 92, 108, 118, 124, 136, and 138

We've listed general questions in an appendix that you can use while studying these psalms.

Week 4

Turn to God in Repentance

Psalms 51 and 53

One of my earliest memories is a winter visit at my cousins' house. I don't recall much about the trip, but one detail is burned into my memory—I was falsely accused. My cousin misheard something I said and told my parents I'd used inappropriate language. My consequence was a long time-out while my brother and cousins played in the snow. It may seem like a silly thing to remember, but it was one of the first times I understood that life isn't always fair.

Decades later, I realize that was an incredibly gentle introduction to a world broken by sin. Sometimes we're sinned against; sometimes we reap the consequences of our own sin; sometimes no one did anything wrong, but life still hurts. As we grapple with life in a sinful and broken world, the Bible offers a special group of psalms to help—laments.

Biblical lament means expressing grief and sorrow to God. Sometimes we lament the results of sin—how it hurts our hearts, minds, bodies, and relationships.

We'll consider that next week. This week, we'll study psalms that lament sin itself, both our personal sin and the sin of others.

 Turn to God in Prayer

Father, sin is within me and all around me. Thank you for your steadfast love and abundant mercy (Ps. 51:1). As I study your word this week, please "teach me wisdom in the secret heart" and help me to turn to you in repentance (Ps. 51:6). In Jesus's name, amen.

 Memory Verse

> Restore to me the joy of your salvation,
>   and uphold me with a willing spirit. (Ps. 51:12)

PSALM 51 OBSERVATION AND INTERPRETATION

Psalm 51

Create in Me a Clean Heart, O God
To the choirmaster. A Psalm of David, when Nathan the prophet went to him, after he had gone in to Bathsheba.

¹ Have mercy on me, O God,
    according to your steadfast love;
  according to your abundant mercy
    blot out my transgressions.
² Wash me thoroughly from my iniquity,
    and cleanse me from my sin!

³ For I know my transgressions,
    and my sin is ever before me.
⁴ Against you, you only, have I sinned
    and done what is evil in your sight,
  so that you may be justified in your words

and blameless in your judgment.
5 Behold, I was brought forth in iniquity,
and in sin did my mother conceive me.
6 Behold, you delight in truth in the inward being,
and you teach me wisdom in the secret heart.

7 Purge me with hyssop, and I shall be clean;
wash me, and I shall be whiter than snow.
8 Let me hear joy and gladness;
let the bones that you have broken rejoice.
9 Hide your face from my sins,
and blot out all my iniquities.
10 Create in me a clean heart, O God,
and renew a right spirit within me.
11 Cast me not away from your presence,
and take not your Holy Spirit from me.
12 Restore to me the joy of your salvation,
and uphold me with a willing spirit.

13 Then I will teach transgressors your ways,
and sinners will return to you.
14 Deliver me from bloodguiltiness, O God,
O God of my salvation,
and my tongue will sing aloud of your righteousness.
15 O Lord, open my lips,
and my mouth will declare your praise.
16 For you will not delight in sacrifice, or I would give it;
you will not be pleased with a burnt offering.
17 The sacrifices of God are a broken spirit;
a broken and contrite heart, O God, you will not despise.

18 Do good to Zion in your good pleasure;
build up the walls of Jerusalem;

> ¹⁹ then will you delight in right sacrifices,
>   in burnt offerings and whole burnt offerings;
>   then bulls will be offered on your altar.

Perhaps like me, you have a story of being falsely accused. When we face an unfair accusation, we try to set the record straight. But how should we respond when someone points out our sin and we know we're guilty? Today we'll begin our study of lament with Psalm 51 and see how David responded in that exact situation. His words not only provide a model of repentance but have a lot to teach us about the nature of sin and the character of God.

Observation: What Does Psalm 51 Say?

Read Psalm 51 and answer the following questions.

1. According to the superscript . . .

   Who came to David?

   _____

   _____

   What had David done?

   _____

   _____

Though this superscript is brief, 2 Samuel 11–12 recounts the full story. David desired a beautiful woman who was married, so he used his position as king to have her husband killed and take her as his wife. These were grievous sins and great misuses of power. God sent the prophet Nathan to confront David, and Psalm 51 records David's response.

TURN TO GOD IN REPENTANCE   101

2. In verses 1–6, David contrasts his character and actions with God's character and actions.

What characteristics of God does David highlight?

List the different ways David describes his sin.

---

3. Read verses 7–12.

In verse 2, David asks God to "wash" and "cleanse" him from sin. List words and phrases in verses 7–10 that add to this imagery.

In verses 10–12, David asks God to act on his behalf in specific ways. Fill in the chart below, noticing what David desires from God.

God's Action	Result for David
Create	A clean heart
Renew	

God's Action	Result for David
Restore	
Uphold	

4. In verses 13–19, David shifts his focus from his current plea for mercy to his future response to the Lord's forgiveness. What are some ways David plans to honor the Lord?

For most of us, admitting we've sinned doesn't come easily. We struggle to utter simple phrases like "I was wrong." David, however, has a lot to say in this psalm. His understanding of repentance seems to involve much more than acknowledging wrongdoing. Now that we're acquainted with Psalm 51, let's begin to consider what it means.

Interpretation: What Does Psalm 51 Mean?

5. The Bible tells us many things about God's character—he is powerful, righteous, just, all-knowing, etc. Why do you think David appeals to God's "steadfast love" and "abundant mercy" before he confesses his sin (v. 1)?

6. As he asks God to address his sin, David uses imagery of cleaning and washing. What might this suggest about the nature of sin and how it affects us?

7. In week 1 we discussed that many psalms are written in chiastic structure, and the main idea of these psalms is found in the middle. This is true of Psalm 51 too. Verses 9–10 help us understand the main idea.

What might be the significance of David asking God to "blot out" his sin? How is blotting out different from covering up?

Why do you think David prayed "create in me a clean heart" instead of "help me not commit murder and adultery"?

David understands that sin isn't just about what we do; it taints everything about who we are. In verses 9–10, David summarizes his (and our) two great needs with regard to sin. We need forgiveness, for God to mercifully blot out our record of wrongs. And because we are sinful from birth, we also need our hearts changed so we can live in obedience to God. Thankfully, God's love is steadfast; it doesn't waver depending on our performance. His mercy is abundant, far greater than our sin. God delights to receive us when we come to him in repentance.

💙 Memory Verse

> Restore to me the joy of your salvation,
> and uphold me with a willing spirit. (Ps. 51:12)

PSALM 51 INTERPRETATION AND APPLICATION

If you've spent much time reading the Bible, you've probably noticed that David isn't the only biblical character who struggled with sin. The problem of sin is introduced just three chapters into the Bible, and the rest of the Bible helps us understand God's plan to solve it. Today we'll look at other passages in both the Old and New Testaments to learn more about the nature of sin and why David turned to God for help.

Interpretation: What Does the Whole Bible Say?

Read Psalm 51 and answer the following questions.

1. Read Jesus's words in Mark 7:21–23.

   What do you think it means that "evil things come from within"?

   _____

   _____

TURN TO GOD IN REPENTANCE 105

How does Jesus's teaching in these verses help us understand the way David describes his sin in Psalm 51?

2. Read Genesis 3:8–10. These verses describe how Adam and Eve hid from God after they ate the forbidden fruit.

How is David's posture toward God after sinning different from Adam and Eve's?

Instead of trying to hide his sin, why do you think David asks God to hide his face (Ps. 51:9)?

3. Read Exodus 34:5–7, where God declares his name to Moses. David would have been familiar with this description of God. How do you think this understanding of God's character might have influenced David's actions after he sinned?

God is holy and no sin can abide in his presence, so when Adam and Eve sinned, they hid in the bushes. But David knew he couldn't do anything to get rid of his sin. So instead of running away, he ran *to* God, trusting in his abundant mercy and steadfast love. Instead of trying to hide himself, David asked God to hide his face.

4. Read 1 John 1:7–10. We usually think of blood as something that stains, not something that cleanses. What might it mean that "the blood of Jesus . . . cleanses us from all sin"?

_____

_____

_____

Hebrews 9:22 says that "without the shedding of blood there is no forgiveness of sins." When Jesus died on the cross, he shed *his* blood to take the punishment for *our* sin. He took all our filthy, dirty sin upon himself so we could be clean and blameless before God. David knew God was the only one who could get rid of his sin, and we know how God did it—he sent Jesus to die on the cross. We don't need to hide from God, trying to cover our sin. We can come to him in repentance like David did, asking God to cleanse us with the shed blood of Jesus.

Application: How Do I Faithfully Respond?

We've spent a lot of time this week considering David's sin and how he confessed it to God. We might be tempted to stop right there and call it a day. It's always easier to think about sin in the context of someone else's life than our own. But laments like Psalm 51 are included in the Bible to help us lament our own sin. So what does it look like for us to turn to God in repentance? Let's apply David's example.

5. When confronted with your sin, is your tendency to confess it or cover it up?

_____

_____

What might this reveal about your view of sin?

What might this reveal about your view of God?

6. David shows us that being honest about our sin is an important step in repentance—"I know my transgressions" (v. 3). What sins do you know you struggle with? What sins have others pointed out to you? If you need help identifying sin, pray that God will teach you "truth in the inward being" (v. 6). Write a prayer below confessing your sin to God and asking him to give you a clean heart.

7. In verses 13–17, we see that the fruit of David's repentance is a change in behavior. Consider the sin you wrote down in question 6. What might it look like for you to turn from that sin and live in obedience to God?

How do you feel after turning to God in repentance? I hope you feel lighter, encouraged that the Lord has blotted out your sin and remembers it no more. But that's not always the case. Sometimes we feel hopeless, frustrated that we keep struggling with the same sin over and over. Sometimes we feel like a fraud, convinced if others knew the sin we confessed, they'd look down on us. Sometimes we feel a right grief that we've dishonored our heavenly Father. Psalm 51 indicates David struggled with some sort of discouragement too. That's why he prayed, "Restore to me the joy of your salvation, / and uphold me with a willing spirit" (v. 12). Make that your prayer as you close your time today.

💙 Memory Verse

> Restore to me the joy of your salvation,
>   and uphold me with a willing spirit. (Ps. 51:12)

PSALM 53 OBSERVATION AND INTERPRETATION

Psalm 53

There Is None Who Does Good

To the choirmaster: according to Mahalath. A Maskil of David.

> 1 The fool says in his heart, "There is no God."
>   They are corrupt, doing abominable iniquity;
>   there is none who does good.
>
> 2 God looks down from heaven
>   on the children of man

to see if there are any who understand,
who seek after God.

3 They have all fallen away;
together they have become corrupt;
there is none who does good,
not even one.

4 Have those who work evil no knowledge,
who eat up my people as they eat bread,
and do not call upon God?

5 There they are, in great terror,
where there is no terror!
For God scatters the bones of him who encamps against you;
you put them to shame, for God has rejected them.

6 Oh, that salvation for Israel would come out of Zion!
When God restores the fortunes of his people,
let Jacob rejoice, let Israel be glad.

Sometimes as we read headlines, scroll through social media feeds, or simply look out our windows, we're discouraged by a culture that seems uninterested, if not hostile, to the things of God. As we've learned, the right response to sin is to turn to God in repentance. But what happens when people continue in their sin instead? How can God's people live faithfully in a world that rejects him?

We'll find help answering these questions in our second psalm of the week, Psalm 53. Like Psalm 51, it's a lament written by David. But instead of looking inward and lamenting his personal sin, David looks outward and laments sin in the world around him. Let's dig in.

Observation: What Does Psalm 53 Say?

Read Psalm 53 and answer the following questions.

1. According to verse 1, what makes a person foolish?

_____

_____

_____

_____

2. Using verses 1–4, fill in the chart below with descriptions of what "the children of man" do and don't do.

What They Do	What They Don't Do
Example: Abominable iniquity (v. 1)	*Example: Good deeds (v. 1)*

3. Verses 5–6 contrast how God responds to those who act against his people with how he will care for his people.

What does God do to those who are against his people (v. 5)?

_____

_____

How will God care for his people (v. 6)?

4. How would you describe the tone (mood or feeling) of verses 1–5? How does the tone change in verse 6?

We have a tendency to look back on the past and think times were better, people were more godly, society was more moral. Of course, there are shifts in norms and values over time. But Psalm 53 reminds us sin has always been pervasive in the world. Thousands of years ago, David lamented that "there is none who does good, / not even one" (v. 3). He describes a culture that denied God's existence and persecuted God's people. Though this psalm was written in David's time, it's incredibly relevant for our time. Let's start to consider what it means.

Interpretation: What Does Psalm 53 Mean?

5. In verse 1, David writes that "there is none who does good," and he repeats the same phrase in verse 3, adding, "not even one." Yet, we all know people who do plenty of good things, whether Christians or not.

What do you think David means?

112 TURN TO GOD IN REPENTANCE

Why might he have written it twice?

6. The first four verses focus on characteristics of people who reject God. But in the middle of these descriptions, David describes God "look[ing] down from heaven on the children of man" (v. 2). Why might David include this image of God as we lament the pervasiveness of sin?

7. In verse 4, David uses the imagery of God's people being eaten up like bread by evildoers. What might this suggest about the effects of sin?

8. For most of Psalm 53, David speaks in present tense as he observes current realities. Why do you think he ends the psalm looking to the future (v. 6)?

Psalms of lament can be hard to read because they articulate dark and discouraging truths about life in a sinful world. On the other hand, we can find great comfort in knowing we're not alone. God's people have navigated these realities for centuries. While David could only look forward with expectant hope that the Lord would one day bring salvation, we can see how God provided that salvation through Jesus. And we look forward to the day when Jesus will come again, putting an end to sin and sorrow forever.

💙 Memory Verse

> Restore to me the joy of your salvation,
>   and uphold me with a willing spirit. (Ps. 51:12)

PSALM 53 INTERPRETATION AND APPLICATION

Have you ever been talking to someone and realized they were telling a story you'd heard before? If you're like me, you might let your mind wander but keep nodding and smiling to avoid being rude. When people repeat themselves, we often don't listen well. But as pastor James Montgomery Boice explains, when God repeats himself, we need to listen carefully:

> Anything God says once demands our attention. Anything he says twice demands our utmost attention. How then if he says something three times, as he does in this case? This demands our keenest concentration, contemplation, assimilation, and even memorization.[1]

Dr. Boice is talking about Psalm 53. It's almost identical to Psalm 14. And in Romans 3, Paul directly quotes Psalm 53. God repeated this same message three times! As we look to other Scripture passages to help us interpret Psalm 53

---

1 James Montgomery Boice, *Psalms: Volume 1* (Baker, 1994), 114.

today, we have the unique advantage of considering how biblical writers used some of the very same verses in different contexts. Let's look carefully at each passage to see what the Lord wants to teach us.

Interpretation: What Does the Whole Bible Say?

1. Read Psalm 14. Psalms 14 and 53 are the same until verses 5–6. The differences seem to indicate Psalm 14 was written to unbelievers as a warning, while Psalm 53 was written to believers as an encouragement.[2] Look carefully at the chart below, which compares these verses side by side. Then answer the questions.

Psalm 14:5–6	Psalm 53:5
There they are in great terror,	There they are, in great terror, where there is no terror!
for God is with the generation of the righteous.	For God scatters the bones of him who encamps against you;
You would shame the plans of the poor, but the LORD is his refuge.	you put them to shame, for God has rejected them.

Both believers and unbelievers may experience "terror" (also translated "dread" or "fear") as they navigate life in a sinful world. What might David mean when he says that for believers "there is no terror"?

_____

_____

2 Timothy and Kathy Keller, *The Songs of Jesus: A Year of Daily Devotions in the Psalms* (Viking, 2015), 114.

In Psalm 53, David assures believers that God will defeat their enemies. How do the parallel verses in Psalm 14 offer additional encouragement for God's people?

2. Read Romans 3:9–20. In this passage, Paul quotes Psalm 53 as he considers some of the similarities and differences between Jews (God's chosen people in the Old Testament) and Gentiles (everyone else).

What do you think Paul wants to convey about Jews and Gentiles by quoting Psalm 53?

Why might God have included this truth that no one is righteous (not even one) three separate times in his word?

3. As we learned in Psalm 51, we are all sinful from birth. By nature, we are all the foolish people David describes in Psalms 14 and 53 who live as if there's no God. Read 1 Corinthians 1:26–30. How can the foolish and wicked become wise and righteous?

4. In verse 6, David looks forward to Israel's salvation and says it will come out of Zion. Read John 12:12–15. Who do you think is the Savior of Zion?

Application: How Do I Faithfully Respond?

David ends Psalm 53 on a hopeful note, but much of the psalm laments sin and evil in a world where many people don't turn to God in repentance. God doesn't expect us to go through life with rose-colored glasses. It's good and right to express sorrow and grief when those around us reject God and don't live according to his ways. And it's good for believers in Christ to remember we were once those people. The more we understand the depth of our sin, the more we'll rejoice in the salvation of God.

5. Consider your community or the larger culture in which you live.

What are some ways you see people living as if there's no God?

When you're confronted with sin and evil in the world, how do you tend to respond: Despair? Fear? Apathy? Judgment? Self-righteousness? How are these responses different from biblical lament?

TURN TO GOD IN REPENTANCE 117

6. How does the reminder that you were once a fool who denied God impact the way you view your unbelieving neighbors? How does it impact the way you view God?

7. At the end of Psalm 53, David turns his focus from present circumstances to future hope of salvation. What are practical ways you could turn your eyes from the world around you and find hope in God's word?

In Psalm 34:15, David writes, "The eyes of the LORD are toward the righteous / and his ears toward their cry." When we turn our eyes to the Lord, we find his eyes already turned toward us, watching over us every moment. We find his ears listening attentively, ready and waiting to hear our cry. When the state of this world tempts you to despair, use the psalms of lament to express your grief to God. But remember, there is no terror for God's people. God sent a Savior out of Zion to defeat our ultimate enemies of sin and death, so we can rejoice and be glad!

💙 Memory Verse

Restore to me the joy of your salvation,
and uphold me with a willing spirit. (Ps. 51:12)

REFLECTION

Apologies are awkward, and many of us prefer to avoid them. But in recent decades, I've noticed a growing willingness to apologize and a desire to do it well. Whether it comes from professional advice in a counseling office or a parenting influencer on social media, we're encouraged to craft specific and unqualified apologies. Something like "I'm sorry *if* you were offended" doesn't cut it. We need to specifically own up to our wrongdoing and how it hurt the other person. I'm all for this—it's biblical and leads to healthier relationships. But we also need to consider our responses.

Nine times out of ten when you apologize to someone, they respond, "It's okay." I understand why that's our default answer. It's efficient and gracious. We can quickly move on from the awkwardness and help the person apologizing feel better. There's just one problem—it's not true. Sin is not okay.

Our sin against one another is not okay, nor is the sin we observe around us. As we saw in Psalm 51, all of it is sin against a holy God. When it comes to personal sin, we'd like to imagine it's not that big of a deal. We can come up with all sorts of reasons to rationalize and explain it. We had a good intention behind it, or we weren't really hurting anyone, or it was so small compared to what others do—*it's okay*.

Perhaps we do the same thing when we look at the world around us. As we noted in our study of Psalm 53, living as God's people in a culture that denies him can lead to fear and despair. But it can also lead to apathy and acceptance. We can become so accustomed to unbiblical beliefs and practices that they don't bother us anymore. We either act as if sin is okay by ignoring it or start to question whether it's sin at all—*maybe it's okay*.

When we act as if sin is okay, we don't do ourselves or anyone else a favor. As our psalms this week showed us, the right response to sin is to turn to God in repentance. We need to be forgiven and made clean by Jesus's blood. If sin were okay, Jesus wouldn't have needed to die on the cross. But the truth is, sin must be punished. So Jesus took that punishment for us, and when he died in our place he didn't say, "It's okay." He said, "It is finished" (John 19:30).

What we need God to say to us when we repent—and what we need to say to each other when we apologize—is "I forgive you." Sin is not okay, but through Jesus's finished work on the cross it can be forgiven. That's why salvation is cause for such joy! The more we understand the depth of our sin, the more deeply we experience the joy of our salvation. Don't skip over the sorrow of sin. Let lament lead you to joy.

1. Why is it important for us to understand that sin is not okay?

2. How do psalms of lament help us think and feel rightly about sin?

💙 Memory Verse

Restore to me the joy of your salvation,
 and uphold me with a willing spirit. (Ps. 51:12)

GROUP DISCUSSION QUESTIONS

Icebreaker: Which emoji do you most frequently use?

Warm-up: What is your typical attitude about sin (avoidance, apathy, fear, guilt, frustration, etc.)?

1. How does the imagery of washing and cleansing help you understand the nature of sin?

2. Why is it important to remember God's abundant mercy and steadfast love when we're confronted with our sin?

TURN TO GOD IN REPENTANCE · 121

3. What is the relationship between heart change and behavior change? What is our role? What is God's role?

4. How can we avoid becoming apathetic about our sin and the sin of those around us?

5. What are some challenges of living as God's people in a sinful world? How can psalms of lament help us navigate these challenges?

6. How are David's prayers for cleansing (Psalm 51) and salvation (Psalm 53) ultimately fulfilled in Jesus?

7. What was one thing that convicted, encouraged, instructed, or stood out to you this week?

8. How did these psalms help you turn your eyes to Jesus?

What did you see or learn about Jesus?

What do you need to believe as a result?

How should you live differently?

♪ Hymn for the Week

"Nothing But the Blood of Jesus"

> What can wash away my sin?
> Nothing but the blood of Jesus.
> What can make me whole again?
> Nothing but the blood of Jesus.
>
> O precious is the flow
> That makes me white as snow;
> No other fount I know;
> Nothing but the blood of Jesus.[3]

Additional Psalms of Lament for Further Study

Psalms 5, 25, 39, 79, 130, and 141

We've listed general questions in an appendix that you can use while studying these psalms.

---

[3] Robert Lowry, "Nothing But the Blood of Jesus," 1876, https://hymnary.org.

Week 5

Turn to God in Suffering

Psalms 102 and 74

Suffering comes in many shapes and sizes. Perhaps we're betrayed by a dear friend or cheated out of a promotion at work. Maybe we receive a scary diagnosis or face the death of a loved one. We might battle chronic illness or struggle with financial hardship. We may have a strained marriage or a wayward child. Sometimes we face more than one of these struggles simultaneously. Because we live in a world broken by sin, no one escapes suffering. The question is, how will we respond when it comes?

When we suffer, there's a temptation to walk away from God. We wonder, *If God is really good, if he really loves me, why would he let this happen?* Or maybe we question whether he exists at all thinking, *If God were real, he would have stopped this*. Suffering can bring up tough questions, but we won't find answers by walking away. As we'll see this week, psalms of lament help us turn to God in suffering, bringing him our grief and hard questions, pleading with him to act on our behalf, and ultimately resting in his character and promises.

Turn to God in Prayer

Father, sometimes life is really painful. It can be hard to see your goodness when bad things happen. Please hear my prayer and let my cry come to you (Ps. 102:1). Help me to trust that you are "working salvation in the midst of the earth" and in the midst of my suffering (Ps. 74:12). In Jesus's name, amen.

Memory Verse

> For the LORD builds up Zion;
>   he appears in his glory;
> he regards the prayer of the destitute
>   and does not despise their prayer. (Ps. 102:16–17)

PSALM 102 OBSERVATION AND INTERPRETATION

Psalm 102

Do Not Hide Your Face from Me
A Prayer of one afflicted, when he is faint and pours out his complaint before the LORD.

> ¹ Hear my prayer, O LORD;
>   let my cry come to you!
> ² Do not hide your face from me
>   in the day of my distress!
> Incline your ear to me;
>   answer me speedily in the day when
>   I call!
>
> ³ For my days pass away like smoke,
>   and my bones burn like a furnace.
> ⁴ My heart is struck down like grass and
>   has withered;
>   I forget to eat my bread.
> ⁵ Because of my loud groaning
>   my bones cling to my flesh.

6 I am like a desert owl of the wilderness,
   like an owl of the waste places;
7 I lie awake;
   I am like a lonely sparrow on the housetop.
8 All the day my enemies taunt me;
   those who deride me use my name for a curse.
9 For I eat ashes like bread
   and mingle tears with my drink,
10 because of your indignation and anger;
   for you have taken me up and thrown me down.
11 My days are like an evening shadow;
   I wither away like grass.

12 But you, O LORD, are enthroned forever;
   you are remembered throughout all generations.
13 You will arise and have pity on Zion;
   it is the time to favor her;
   the appointed time has come.
14 For your servants hold her stones dear
   and have pity on her dust.
15 Nations will fear the name of the LORD,
   and all the kings of the earth will fear your glory.
16 For the LORD builds up Zion;
   he appears in his glory;
17 he regards the prayer of the destitute
   and does not despise their prayer.

18 Let this be recorded for a generation to come,
   so that a people yet to be created may praise the LORD:
19 that he looked down from his holy height;
   from heaven the LORD looked at the earth,
20 to hear the groans of the prisoners,
   to set free those who were doomed to die,
21 that they may declare in Zion the name of the LORD,
   and in Jerusalem his praise,

22 when peoples gather together,
  and kingdoms, to worship the LORD.

23 He has broken my strength in midcourse;
  he has shortened my days.
24 "O my God," I say, "take me not away
  in the midst of my days—
you whose years endure
  throughout all generations!"

25 Of old you laid the foundation of the earth,
  and the heavens are the work of your hands.
26 They will perish, but you will remain;
  they will all wear out like a garment.
You will change them like a robe, and they will pass away,
27   but you are the same, and your years have no end.
28 The children of your servants shall dwell secure;
  their offspring shall be established before you.

When we're suffering, it can be hard to pray. Maybe we can't find the words to express our thoughts and feelings, or we're afraid that what we really think might not be appropriate to say to God. That's why I love the psalms of lament. They give us vulnerable and honest words to express our suffering. And because they're part of God's holy, inspired word, we can be confident they'll help us rightly approach the Lord.

Unlike several of the psalms we've studied, Psalm 102 doesn't name its author. Instead, the superscript says, "A prayer of one afflicted, when he is faint and pours out his complaint before the Lord." Whether we're suffering now, have suffered in the past, or will suffer in the future, we're all the "afflicted one" at some point, and Psalm 102 can help us turn to God. If you're not currently in a season of suffering, let this psalm give you compassion for those who are and prepare you to suffer well in the future.

Observation: What Does Psalm 102 Say?

Read Psalm 102 and answer the following questions.

1. Remember that psalms often use parallelism, repeating the same idea in different ways to emphasize a point. In verses 1–2, how would you summarize what the psalmist wants God to do?

2. In verses 3–11, the psalmist uses figurative language to describe his suffering. His descriptions generally fit in one of three categories: physical, emotional, or relational suffering. Fill in the chart below with phrases from these verses that represent each type.

Physical Suffering	Emotional Suffering	Relational Suffering

3. The tone of Psalm 102 shifts in verse 12 as the psalmist turns from reflecting on his own situation and looks to the Lord—"But you, O LORD . . ." What characteristic of God is highlighted in verses 12, 24, and 27?

4. The psalmist also shifts from focusing on his needs to praying for others' needs.

   Why does the psalmist want a written record of how God delivered his people from suffering (v. 18)?

   What final hope does the psalmist express in verse 28?

Interpretation: What Does Psalm 102 Mean?

5. In Psalm 139, David explains that God knows everything about us and everything that happens to us. Yet in Psalm 102, the psalmist spends numerous verses (vv. 3–11) explaining his suffering to God.

   Why might the psalmist tell God things God already knows?

What do you think this suggests about God's posture toward people who suffer?

6. Why do you think the psalmist meditates on God's eternal nature—that he endures through all generations (v. 24) and remains when everything else passes away (v. 26)—amid his suffering?

7. In verses 12–22, the psalmist confidently describes how the Lord will show mercy to his people in the future.

Why do you think the psalmist turns from focusing on his individual story to considering the story of God's people?

Why might the psalmist focus on what God will do in the future even though he is suffering in the present?

As we move through Psalm 102, we see different phases of the psalmist processing his suffering. He begins describing his anguish to the Lord as he grapples with the brevity of life. He demonstrates that it's good and right for us to tell the Lord about our troubles. Like the psalmist, we'll find in him a listening ear.

But the psalmist doesn't stop there, drowning in his sorrows. He lifts his eyes and looks to the Lord, remembering God's eternal nature and faithful care for his people. Regardless of how the psalmist's situation ends, he's confident that God's people and promises will prevail. As the psalmist considers his circumstances as part God's larger story of redemption, he finds hope—and so can we.

💙 Memory Verse

> For the LORD builds up Zion;
>   he appears in his glory;
> he regards the prayer of the destitute
>   and does not despise their prayer. (Ps. 102:16–17)

PSALM 102 INTERPRETATION AND APPLICATION

One of the greatest comforts we have in suffering is knowing we're not alone. Whether it's finding someone else who has suffered in a similar way and can relate, or simply having someone by our side as a loving, supportive presence, we tend to find hope through connection. Similarly, the afflicted one writing Psalm 102 takes comfort in knowing he doesn't suffer alone. Today we'll explore other Scripture passages that show how the psalmist connects his suffering to other suffering believers and to God's ultimate work of redemption in Christ.

Interpretation: What Does the Whole Bible Say?

Read Psalm 102 and answer the following questions.

1. In verses 1–2, the psalmist calls out to God with wording we find in other psalms. Review the chart below that compares Psalm 102:1–2 with other similar verses. Then answer the questions that follow.

Psalm 102	Other Psalms
v. 1 Hear my prayer, O LORD; / let my cry come to you!	39:12 Hear my prayer, O LORD, / and give ear to my cry.
v. 2 Do not hide your face from me.	27:9 Hide not your face from me.
v. 2 In the day of my distress!	18:6 In my distress I called upon the LORD.
v. 2 Incline your ear to me.	71:2 Incline your ear to me, and save me!
v. 2 Answer me speedily in the day when I call!	69:17 Make haste to answer me.

Why do you think the writer of Psalm 102 used language similar to earlier psalms as he wrote his lament?

What might the repetition of similar phrases in psalms of lament suggest about the nature of suffering?

2. In verses 12–22, the psalmist finds hope in considering how God will restore Zion and free his people to worship him there. In Scripture, Zion often refers to the city of Jerusalem, the center of Israel's kingdom and location of the temple. In these verses, the psalmist seems to be looking forward to God restoring Jerusalem after a particular enemy attack, but he also foreshadows a greater restoration to come. Read Revelation 21:1–4.

How is the new Jerusalem the ultimate answer to the psalmist's prayer?

How might looking forward to the new Jerusalem offer hope amid current suffering?

3. Read Hebrews 1:1–12, noticing how the writer of Hebrews quotes Psalm 102:25–27.

According to this passage from Hebrews, who is the psalmist describing in verses 25–27?

How does Jesus's eternal nature give us hope as we suffer?

When we suffer, it can be tempting to isolate ourselves, thinking no one understands. While the details of our suffering may be unique, the experience of suffering is common to humanity—and so is the answer to our suffering. The afflicted one writing Psalm 102 joins his voice with other suffering psalmists because he knows he needs to turn to the Lord in his suffering just like they have.[1]

He also understands that God's response to his suffering is part of a larger story of God caring for his people. Though our suffering may seem never-ending, only God is eternal. And he's working all things for the good of his people as we move toward that final day when he will return and undo death and suffering forever.

Application: How Do I Faithfully Respond?

4. When you suffer, do you tend to turn *to* God or *away* from him? Why?

5. Think of a specific situation of suffering in your life now, even if it seems minor.

What are the circumstances of your suffering?

---

1   James M. Hamilton Jr., *Psalms Volume II* (Lexham Academic, 2021), 218.

Write a verse from this psalm that describes how you feel amid this suffering (see vv. 3–11 and 23–24).

Write a verse that reminds you of God's faithfulness to his people (see vv. 12–22 and 28).

Write a verse that gives you hope or comfort in God's character and work (see vv. 12–17 and 24–27).

6. Use your answers in question 5 to help you write a prayer on the lines below telling God about your suffering, asking him for help, and expressing trust in his faithfulness.

God doesn't always answer our prayers for relief from suffering the way we'd like. Some relationships remain strained, some sicknesses end in death, and some desires are left unfulfilled. But that's not because God isn't listening or doesn't care. Psalm 102 assures us that God regards our prayers and works all things for the eternal good of his people. When our individual circumstances are hard, when sin and death seem to be winning, we look forward to the day when sin and death will be no more and God himself will wipe away every tear from our eyes.

 **Memory Verse**

> For the LORD builds up Zion;
>   he appears in his glory;
> he regards the prayer of the destitute
>   and does not despise their prayer. (Ps. 102:16–17)

PSALM 74 OBSERVATION AND INTERPRETATION

Psalm 74

Arise, O God, Defend Your Cause
A Maskil of Asaph.

> 1 O God, why do you cast us off forever?
>   Why does your anger smoke against
>   the sheep of your pasture?
> 2 Remember your congregation, which
>   you have purchased of old,
>   which you have redeemed to be the
>   tribe of your heritage!
>   Remember Mount Zion, where you
>   have dwelt.
> 3 Direct your steps to the perpetual ruins;
>   the enemy has destroyed everything
>   in the sanctuary!
>
> 4 Your foes have roared in the midst of
>   your meeting place;
>   they set up their own signs for signs.
> 5 They were like those who swing axes
>   in a forest of trees.

6 And all its carved wood
   they broke down with hatchets and hammers.
7 They set your sanctuary on fire;
   they profaned the dwelling place of your name,
   bringing it down to the ground.
8 They said to themselves, "We will utterly subdue them";
   they burned all the meeting places of God in the land.

9 We do not see our signs;
   there is no longer any prophet,
   and there is none among us who knows how long.
10 How long, O God, is the foe to scoff?
   Is the enemy to revile your name forever?
11 Why do you hold back your hand, your right hand?
   Take it from the fold of your garment and destroy them!

12 Yet God my King is from of old,
   working salvation in the midst of the earth.
13 You divided the sea by your might;
   you broke the heads of the sea monsters on the waters.
14 You crushed the heads of Leviathan;
   you gave him as food for the creatures of the wilderness.
15 You split open springs and brooks;
   you dried up ever-flowing streams.
16 Yours is the day, yours also the night;
   you have established the heavenly lights and the sun.
17 You have fixed all the boundaries of the earth;
   you have made summer and winter.

18 Remember this, O LORD, how the enemy scoffs,
   and a foolish people reviles your name.
19 Do not deliver the soul of your dove to the wild beasts;
   do not forget the life of your poor forever.

^{20} Have regard for the covenant,
　　for the dark places of the land are full of the habitations of violence.
^{21} Let not the downtrodden turn back in shame;
　　let the poor and needy praise your name.

^{22} Arise, O God, defend your cause;
　　remember how the foolish scoff at you all the day!
^{23} Do not forget the clamor of your foes,
　　the uproar of those who rise against you, which goes up continually!

If you've ever tried on clothes labeled "one size fits all," you probably realized they don't fit anyone particularly well. People come in different shapes and sizes, and as we mentioned at the beginning of the week, so does suffering. Thankfully, the psalms don't take a "one size fits all" approach to lament.

Today we turn to our second psalm of the week, Psalm 74. Instead of coming from the perspective of an individual, it's a corporate lament about the collective suffering of God's people, and it takes a different tone and approach than Psalm 102. But we'll find its purpose is the same—to help God's people turn to him in suffering.

Observation: What Does Psalm 74 Say?

Read Psalm 74 and answer the following questions.

1. Psalm 102 is primarily written in statements, but Psalm 74 includes questions. What does the psalmist ask God in the verses below?

Verse 1

Verse 10

Verse 11

2. Psalm 74 also includes many calls for God to act on behalf of his people. What does the psalmist want God to do in the verses below?

Verse 2

Verse 11

Verse 20

3. Verses 3–8 describe the particular sufferings God's people have endured at the hands of their enemies. What has happened to the sanctuary/meeting place?

4. In verses 12–17, the psalmist shifts from describing the enemy's destruction to describing God's character and works.

What is God "working" according to verse 12?

What characteristic of God is noted in verse 13 and supported by the examples in verses 14–15?

In Psalm 102, we heard from a psalmist who was downcast and discouraged. In Psalm 74, we find a different tone. The psalmist starts right from the first verse with impassioned questions: *Why aren't you intervening on behalf of your people, God? How long are you going to let this go on? Why are you letting the enemy get away with this?*

As we mentioned previously, suffering often brings up hard questions. Psalm 74 shows us where we can take them—straight to God. The psalmist demonstrates that we can not only bring him our questions, we can lay out our arguments for why he should answer. Let's take a closer look at the psalmist's arguments.

Interpretation: What Does Psalm 74 Mean?

5. Numerous times in this psalm, we find pleas for God to "remember" or "not forget" his people (vv. 2, 18, 19, 22, 23). What might this suggest about how God's people felt amid their suffering?

6. In verses 1–11, the psalmist explains why God's people need salvation. Why do you think the next section (vv. 12–17) describes examples of God's power and might?

7. In verse 22, the psalmist says, "Arise, O God, defend your cause." It's one of many places where the psalmist uses the word *your*—"your congregation" and "your heritage" (v. 2), "your foes" and "your meeting place" (v. 4), "your poor" (v. 19) and "your name" (v. 21). Why might the psalmist emphasize that all this belongs to the Lord?

8. Some psalms, like Psalm 102, end on a different note than they began. Psalm-ists often come to God with a problem and end with hope in his promises. Psalm 74, however, ends pretty much the way it started—with pleas for God to save his people. How does Psalm 74 add to our understanding of what it looks like to come to God in lament?

In Psalm 74, we find the psalmist coming to the Lord in frustration, asking hard questions about why he's not intervening and laying out an argument for why God should defend his people. In his commentary on this psalm, Dr. James Montgomery Boice encourages us to follow Asaph's model. "Make a list of why God should answer your prayer and plead those reasons," he writes. "Either God will answer, or you will find that your prayer is not a good one and you will pray for something better."[2] Prayer isn't just about what God can do *for* us, it's also about what God does *in* us. Sometimes he changes our circumstances, and sometimes he changes our hearts.

💙 Memory Verse

> For the LORD builds up Zion;
>   he appears in his glory;
> he regards the prayer of the destitute
>   and does not despise their prayer. (Ps. 102:16–17)

---

2 James Montgomery Boice, *Psalms: Volume 2* (Baker, 1996), 622.

PSALM 74 INTERPRETATION AND APPLICATION

If you're like me, you probably imagine something negative when you hear the word *argument*. You might think of an angry dispute or a child disrespectfully talking back to an adult. But when we think of Psalm 74 as an argument, it's more helpful to think in terms of a court case. Attorneys present an argument, or a set of reasons, to convince a judge to make a particular ruling. Arguments may be presented with passion and urgency, but always with a great deal of respect for the judge's authority. Keep that picture in mind today as we continue to explore the psalmist's arguments by looking to other passages of Scripture.

Interpretation: What Does the Whole Bible Say?

1. Psalm 74 isn't the only place in Scripture where we find someone presenting an argument to God. Let's consider a time when a woman made her case to Jesus and see how he responded. Read Matthew 15:21–28.

   After the woman presented her argument to Jesus, what did he praise about her?

   _____

   _____

   How do you think the psalmist's arguments in Psalm 74 demonstrate faith in God?

   _____

   _____

2. In verse 10, the psalmist asks a question we find in many other psalms: "How long, O God . . . ?" When we suffer, we want to know when it will end, and it can be hard to understand why God doesn't fix it right away.

Read 2 Peter 3:8–9. Why might the Lord take a long time (in our view) to put an end to his enemies?

Read Romans 5:3–5. Why do you think God allows his people to suffer, sometimes for a long time, when he has the power to stop it immediately?

3. In verse 11, the psalmist asks God to destroy the enemy, and we find similar requests in other psalms, sometimes with even more graphic details. Even though we know the psalms are written for us to use as prayers, we may wonder if it's okay to repeat such a request. Read Romans 12:19.

Whose job is it to punish evil?

How might the psalmist's request in verse 11 be a way of honoring Romans 12:19?

146 TURN TO GOD IN SUFFERING

4. In verse 20, the psalmist pleads with God to "have regard for the covenant." In the Bible, a covenant is a relationship that God establishes with his people and guarantees by his word.[3]

Read Genesis 12:1–3, where God makes a covenant with Abraham. Based on what God promises in these verses, what might the psalmist mean when says, "Have regard for the covenant" in Psalm 74:20?

_____

_____

Read Galatians 3:29. How can God's covenant with Abraham be applied to us?

_____

_____

Charles Spurgeon called this appeal about the covenant the "master-key" of the psalm. "Heaven's gate must open to this," he wrote. "God is not a man that he should lie; his covenant he will not break."[4] Ultimately, God's covenant promises in the Old Testament are fulfilled in Jesus Christ and applied to all who are in him.

If we're in Christ, this is the hope we have when we suffer—God will not break his promises. Either now or in eternity, they will be fulfilled to the last detail. It's good and right for God's people to ask him to fulfill his covenant promises. Bringing our argument to God in this way isn't disrespectful; it's an act of faith.

Application: How Do I Faithfully Respond?

5. Remember that Psalm 74 is a corporate lament, helping God's people turn to him in suffering together. When you encounter suffering, do you tend to

---

3 *First Catechism: Teaching Children Bible Truths* (Great Commission Publications, 2003), 10.
4 Charles Spurgeon, *The Treasury of David: Volume 2* (Zondervan, 1976), 278.

withdraw from others or move toward them? How can staying in community with other believers help us when we suffer?

6. The writer of Psalm 74 clearly doesn't like the circumstances God has allowed, but instead of turning away in anger or self-pity, he brings his questions and arguments to the Lord.

Describe a situation where you'd like God to intervene on behalf of his people. It might involve your local church, your community, or believers around the world. Consider situations of injustice, church conflict, unmet needs, etc.

What questions do you want to ask God about this situation?

What aspects of God's character and promises give you hope that God will act in this situation?

Write down the name(s) of one or more fellow believers you can ask to pray with you about this situation.

_____

_____

Using your answers, write a prayer on the lines below, making your argument to God and asking him to intervene.

_____

_____

_____

_____

_____

_____

Though the world seeks to tear down the church, the Lord builds up his people (Ps. 102:16). In Christ we're brought into God's covenant family of believers across generations and around the globe. There are corporate laments because God intends for his people to seek him together. We're not meant to navigate suffering or the Christian life alone.

💙 Memory Verse

> For the LORD builds up Zion;
>   he appears in his glory;
> he regards the prayer of the destitute
>   and does not despise their prayer. (Ps. 102:16–17)

REFLECTION

Have you ever been completely sure of something only to find out later you were dead wrong? I'm embarrassed to admit I went almost a year convinced I was thirty-eight when I was only thirty-seven. I have no idea how I could have been wrong about my own age. But when I did the math, I knew the numbers couldn't lie. What I felt was right had to submit to what was objectively true. And thankfully, the truth was good news—I was younger than I thought!

That's a silly example, but the principle is important—what we feel isn't always the same as what's true. In Psalm 74, we noticed the psalmist pleads with God to "remember" over and over. I don't know if the psalmist truly believed God had forgotten his people, but this repeated cry suggests God's people likely *felt* forgotten. And we find similar feelings expressed in other passages like Isaiah 49, where God's people say, "The LORD has forsaken me; / my Lord has forgotten me" (v. 14).

But the Lord assures them it's not only untrue that he's forgotten them—it's impossible. "Can a woman forget her nursing child, / that she should have no compassion on the son of her womb?" God asks. "Even these may forget, / yet I will not forget you" (v. 15). God presents the most unlikely situation we can imagine—a mother forgetting her nursing child—and he says, *Even if that could happen, I still wouldn't forget you.*

It's an amazing promise, and part of what makes it so comforting is the context. God's people felt the Lord had forgotten them, which was completely untrue, but he didn't strike them down for their false accusation or reprimand them for being disrespectful. No, he tenderly reassured them. God's people voiced their honest feelings, and he gave them a beautiful assurance of his love.

When we suffer, we may feel forgotten, hopeless, alone, or betrayed. But our feelings aren't the best indicator of reality. We need to come to the Lord and lay our feelings beside the truth of his word.

Do you feel forgotten? God says, "I will not forget you" (Isa. 49:15). Do you feel alone? God says, "I will be with you" (Isa. 43:2). Do you feel helpless? God says, "I will strengthen you, I will help you, / I will uphold you with my righteous right hand" (Isa. 41:10). Whatever you feel in your suffering, turn to the Lord and tell him about it. Meditate on the truth of who God is in the pages of his word and find hope.

1. How do you feel amid your suffering? How do your feelings compare with the truth of God's word?

2. What's one truth about God that gives you hope today?

💙 Memory Verse

> For the Lord builds up Zion;
>   he appears in his glory;
> he regards the prayer of the destitute
>   and does not despise their prayer. (Ps. 102:16–17)

GROUP DISCUSSION QUESTIONS

Icebreaker: What's one of the best sad songs or movies you've heard or seen?

Warm-up: How has another person helped or encouraged you in a time of suffering?

1. How does remembering the larger story of God redeeming his people change our perspective on individual suffering?

2. Why do the psalmists describe their suffering to God when he already knows what's happening to them? What does this suggest about God's character?

3. How does God use suffering for our good? What is our ultimate hope when suffering persists in this life?

4. What does it mean to bring an argument to God? How can this be an act of faith?

5. Why is it important to remember God's covenant promises when we suffer?

6. What are some questions you have about suffering? How did the psalms this week help you begin to answer them?

7. What was one thing that convicted, encouraged, instructed, or stood out to you this week?

8. How did these psalms help you turn your eyes to Jesus?

What did you see or learn about Jesus?

What do you need to believe as a result?

How should you live differently?

♪ Hymn for the Week

"It Is Well with My Soul"

> When peace like a river attendeth my way,
> When sorrows like sea billows roll;
> Whatever my lot, thou hast taught me to say,
> It is well, it is well with my soul.
>
> It is well (It is well)
> With my soul; (with my soul)
> It is well, it is well with my soul.[5]

Additional Psalms of Lament for Suffering for Further Study

Psalms 13, 22, 28, 42, 43, 55, 56, and 63

We've listed general questions in an appendix that you can use while studying these psalms.

---

5 Horatio Gates Spafford, "When Peace, Like a River," 1873, https://hymnary.org.

Week 6

Turn to God as King

Psalms 72 and 110

Something in the human heart longs for righteousness and justice. It's what makes us hate the evil stepmother in *Cinderella*, cringe when Prince Humperdinck tortures Westley in *The Princess Bride*, and cheer when Simba throws Scar off the cliff's edge in *The Lion King*. We all long to live in a world where goodness triumphs and human flourishing prevails.

Yet for all sorts of reasons, injustice remains. We often look to our leaders for help. We desire those in authority to provide peace, prosperity, and human flourishing. This is why Israel longed for and prayed for a king who would serve the people instead of oppressing them, who would rule with power and conquer their enemies, and who would make their land a conduit of blessing to the rest of the world. Their prayers suggest they expected an answer in the form of an earthly king, but no earthly king—not even Israel's greatest king, David—could accomplish the transformation they wanted. They needed a godly king whose reign would never end.

This week we turn to royal psalms, which often describe the Davidic monarchy but ultimately find their culmination in Jesus Christ's eternal kingdom. Royal (or kingly) psalms celebrate Israel's king as the one who represents God's righteous reign on earth. Through our study we will see that Jesus is the fulfillment of the psalmist's hope. He is God's chosen King who will rule over us in a kingdom where justice reigns forever. Jesus is the King our hearts long for.

 Turn to God in Prayer

Father, I long to live in a place where justice reigns and evil is impossible. As I study, please turn my eyes to King Jesus, the righteous judge whose kingdom is eternal. In Christ's name I pray, amen.

Memory Verse

> Give the king your justice, O God,
>   and your righteousness to the royal son! (Ps. 72:1)

PSALM 72 OBSERVATION AND INTERPRETATION

Psalm 72

Give the King Your Justice
Of Solomon.

> ¹ Give the king your justice, O God,
>   and your righteousness to the
>   royal son!
> ² May he judge your people with
>   righteousness,
>   and your poor with justice!
> ³ Let the mountains bear prosperity for
>   the people,
>   and the hills, in righteousness!
> ⁴ May he defend the cause of the poor of
>   the people,

give deliverance to the children of the needy,
and crush the oppressor!

5   May they fear you while the sun endures,
and as long as the moon, throughout all generations!
6   May he be like rain that falls on the mown grass,
like showers that water the earth!
7   In his days may the righteous flourish,
and peace abound, till the moon be no more!

8   May he have dominion from sea to sea,
and from the River to the ends of the earth!
9   May desert tribes bow down before him,
and his enemies lick the dust!
10   May the kings of Tarshish and of the coastlands
render him tribute;
may the kings of Sheba and Seba
bring gifts!
11   May all kings fall down before him,
all nations serve him!

12   For he delivers the needy when he calls,
the poor and him who has no helper.
13   He has pity on the weak and the needy,
and saves the lives of the needy.
14   From oppression and violence he redeems their life,
and precious is their blood in his sight.

15   Long may he live;
may gold of Sheba be given to him!
May prayer be made for him continually,
and blessings invoked for him all the day!

16 May there be abundance of grain in the land;
　　on the tops of the mountains may it wave;
　　may its fruit be like Lebanon;
and may people blossom in the cities
　　like the grass of whe field!
17 May his name endure forever,
　　his fame continue as long as the sun!
May people be blessed in him,
　　all nations call him blessed!

18 Blessed be the LORD, the God of Israel,
　　who alone does wondrous things.
19 Blessed be his glorious name forever;
　　may the whole earth be filled with his glory!
　　Amen and Amen!

20 The prayers of David, the son of Jesse, are ended.

It's difficult to thrive under poor leadership. But when a person in authority over you has integrity, skill, and strength, you're free to flourish. Today we'll begin studying Psalm 72 in which the author, probably David, prays that the king succeeding him will lead with righteousness and justice so that Israel will be fruitful. Though Israel had a few good kings throughout their history, we'll see that only Christ can truly fulfill this psalm and bring about the eternal kingdom the Old Testament promises.

Observation: What Does Psalm 72 Say?

Read Psalm 72 and mark the following key words and phrases and their synonyms: *righteousness,* *"may he,"* *poor* or *needy,* *blessed,* and *forever.* Then answer the following questions.

1. The author of this psalm prays for the king. For each set of verses, write a brief summary of the prayer request. The first is done for you as an example.

Verses	Prayer Request
vv. 1–3	*May the king rule with righteousness.*
v. 4	
vv. 5–7	
vv. 8–11	
vv. 15–17	

2. How does the king care for the poor and needy?

3. List the words and phrases in this psalm that describe the length of the king's reign.

Each of the five books of the Psalter closes with a doxology. A doxology is a statement of praise that normally appears at the end of a prayer or hymn. Bible scholars have determined verses 18–20 were not originally part of Psalm 72 but are instead the doxology for Book 2. The table below shows the doxology that closes each book of the Psalter.

Book of the Psalter	Doxology
Book 1	Blessed be the Lord, the God of Israel, from everlasting to everlasting! Amen and Amen. (Ps. 41:13)
Book 2	Blessed be the Lord, the God of Israel, who alone does wondrous things. Blessed be his glorious name forever; may the whole earth be filled with his glory! Amen and Amen! (Ps. 72:18–19)
Book 3	Blessed be the Lord forever! Amen and Amen. (Ps. 89:52)

Book of the Psalter	Doxology

Book 4	Blessed be the LORD, the God of Israel,
	    from everlasting to everlasting!
	And let all the people say, "Amen!"
	    Praise the LORD! (Ps. 106:48)

Book 5	Let everything that has breath praise the LORD! Praise the LORD! (Ps. 150:6)

4. Read the doxologies and answer the following questions.

How are the doxologies similar?

How are the doxologies different?

How long will the king of Psalm 72 reign?

Whether the last few verses of Psalm 72 are part of the psalm or a separate doxology, the point is the same: Blessed be the Lord whose kingdom has no end!

Interpretation: What Does Psalm 72 Mean?

5. In Psalm 72:1–2, why does the psalmist pray that the king would reign in justice and righteousness?

6. In Psalm 72:5–7, the author uses imagery from nature (sun, moon, and rain) to describe the king and his reign. What do you think this conveys about the king who fulfills Psalm 72? In what ways should his reign affect the people's lives?

7. The psalmist mentions deliverance for the poor and needy in verse 4 and then returns to this idea in verses 12–14. Why do you think the psalmist emphasizes this aspect of the king's reign?

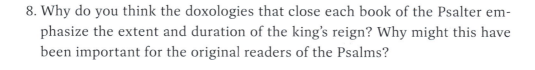

8. Why do you think the doxologies that close each book of the Psalter emphasize the extent and duration of the king's reign? Why might this have been important for the original readers of the Psalms?

God's original plan was to bless the entire world through his chosen people. And the author of Psalm 72 pleads with God to bring his promise to pass through an earthly king. But tomorrow we will see that no earthly king would suffice. The world needed a righteous king who would reign forever.

💙 **Memory Verse**

> Give the king your justice, O God,
>   and your righteousness to the royal son! (Ps. 72:1)

PSALM 72 INTERPRETATION AND APPLICATION

When reading psalms it's important to consider both their near and future fulfillment. The author of Psalm 72 prays that Israel would have a righteous king in his day who would bless the people, but this psalm also points to a future king. In this lesson we'll consider additional scriptures to help us to identify the eternal King and explore what this psalm means for us today. Begin your study time with prayer asking God to show you amazing things in his word.

Interpretation: What Does the Whole Bible Say?

1. Early in Israel's history, God promised to bless his people for their obedience. Read Deuteronomy 28:1–14. How is the life described in this passage similar to the one prayed for in Psalm 72?

For the three hundred years after King David died, Israel experienced life under many evil kings who oppressed the people and caused great suffering in the land. None of these kings could perfectly fulfill Psalm 72 because even the best king could still provide only temporary prosperity. So, Psalm 72 points forward to a better king.

2. In 2 Samuel 7, God promised David he would always have a son on the throne. In other words, the Davidic kingdom would never end! Read Matthew 1:1–16. How does Christ's genealogy help identify Jesus as the fulfillment of God's promise to Abraham and David?

3. The author of Psalm 72 prays that the king would have dominion "from sea to sea" (v. 8), that all *other* "kings" would fall down before him (v. 11), and that his kingdom of righteousness and peace would last as long as creation

(vv. 5–7). Read the passages below and explain how each points to Jesus as the fulfillment of these prayers.

John 14:27

Luke 1:26–33

Galatians 3:7–14

Philippians 2:5–11

Psalm 72 is completely fulfilled in Christ Jesus! He is the righteous man described in Psalm 1 and the royal king of Psalm 2. His reign will never end. He is the King of kings.

Application: How Do I Faithfully Respond?

4. The author of Psalm 72 longed for a better king—one who would judge the people with righteousness and bring blessing to all. But no earthly king will ever do this perfectly.

166 TURN TO GOD AS KING

What is an appropriate expectation for what government leaders can provide? How are you tempted to look to your government or leaders to provide ultimate peace and prosperity?

How might Psalm 72 help you pray for your leaders while still placing your hope for true justice and righteousness in Christ alone?

5. When we read that the king of Psalm 72 delivers the needy, we're meant to reflect on our own response to the poor. How does this psalm prompt you to pray for the poor and needy? What might you do this week to serve those who are suffering?

6. Psalm 72 shows us that Jesus deserves our reverence (v. 5), allegiance (v. 8), and worship (v. 11). What would it look like for King Jesus to receive all your reverence, allegiance, and worship?

7. Psalm 72 teaches us what life will be like after Jesus returns and establishes his forever kingdom. How might singing the truths of this psalm encourage you while you wait?

 **Memory Verse**

> Give the king your justice, O God,
>   and your righteousness to the royal son! (Ps. 72:1)

PSALM 110 OBSERVATION AND INTERPRETATION

Psalm 110

Sit at My Right Hand
A Psalm of David.

> ¹ The LORD says to my Lord:
>   "Sit at my right hand,
>   until I make your enemies your footstool."
>
> ² The LORD sends forth from Zion
>   your mighty scepter.
>   Rule in the midst of your enemies!
> ³ Your people will offer themselves freely
>   on the day of your power,
>   in holy garments;
> from the womb of the morning,
>   the dew of your youth will be yours.

4 The LORD has sworn
and will not change his mind,
"You are a priest forever
after the order of Melchizedek."

5 The Lord is at your right hand;
he will shatter kings on the day of his wrath.
6 He will execute judgment among the nations,
filling them with corpses;
he will shatter chiefs
over the wide earth.
7 He will drink from the brook by the way;
therefore he will lift up his head.

We continue our study of royal psalms today by turning to Psalm 110, the New Testament's most frequently quoted psalm. While Psalm 72 had both a near and a future fulfillment, this Davidic psalm is primarily focused on the future king. Through our study today we will be introduced to a significant Old Testament character whose identity reveals something amazing about God's plan to redeem a people for himself. Before you jump in, pray that God will open your eyes to see Christ as the only true King.

Observation: What Does Psalm 110 Say?

Read Psalm 110 and answer the following questions.

1. This psalm is divided into two oracles (or sacred messages) from God (the LORD) to the Davidic king (my Lord). What does God say in each of the following verses?

Verse 1

Verse 4

2. According to verses 1–2, what will happen to the king's enemies?

3. Read verses 3–5. Oftentimes in Scripture, "the day" refers to the future day of judgment (Joel 1:15; Amos 5:18; Rom. 2:5; Rev. 6:15–17). What words and phrases does the psalmist use to describe "the day" in the following verses:

Verse 3

Verse 5

170 ❖ TURN TO GOD AS KING

4. Read verse 4.

What other office does this king hold?

_____

_____

What additional character is introduced in this verse and what is said
about him?

_____

_____

5. According to verses 5–7, what five things will the king do?

He will . . . _____

He will . . . _____

He will . . . _____

He will . . . _____

He will . . . _____

Psalm 1 and Psalm 2 are known as a gateway to the Psalter. Earlier this week
we saw that the king of Psalm 72 is the blessed man of Psalm 1. In Psalm 2 the
focus is on God's anointed king—one who "sits in the heavens," (Ps. 2:4), reigns
from Zion (v. 6), and breaks enemy nations with a rod of iron (vv. 8–9). Notice
the similar language and imagery used in Psalm 110 as we turn now to consider
the meaning of this psalm.

Interpretation: What Does Psalm 110 Mean?

6. "God's right hand" is a place of honor and power. Why do you think God mentions the "right hand" in both of this psalm's oracles (v. 1 and v. 5)?

7. In verses 5–6 we read that the king will "shatter kings," "execute judgment," and fill the nations with corpses. What does this imagery convey about the future of God's enemies?

8. The first oracle of Psalm 110 is directed to a king, but in verse 4 this king is called a priest. Tomorrow we'll learn much more about Melchizedek, the mysterious and highly significant historical figure here, but for now, consider the differences between a king and a priest. Why might it be odd for one man to be both?

God promised David that one of his descendants would reign forever, so we aren't surprised when we read in Psalm 110 about the Davidic king who will rule from Zion (the symbolic representation of God's presence with his people on earth) and sit at God's right hand. However, the original readers of this psalm would have been shocked to learn this king would also be a priest (Ps. 110:4)! In the Old Testament, the offices of king and priest were distinct, and their respective duties were not to be conflated. To understand this psalm, we must learn more about Melchizedek and his unique role as priest. That's what we'll do tomorrow, but for now, reflect on the truth that God's forever king is unlike any other.

💙 Memory Verse

> Give the king your justice, O God,
> and your righteousness to the royal son! (Ps. 72:1)

PSALM 110 INTERPRETATION AND APPLICATION

Today we finally get to uncover the mystery surrounding Melchizedek! We'll also look at other passages that help us understand Psalm 110's meaning. Before you begin, read Psalm 110 and pray that the Lord would shine his light of understanding into your heart and mind.

Interpretation: What Does the Whole Bible Say?

1. The "right hand" of God is mentioned more than 140 times in Scripture! Moses referred to it in the song he sang after the exodus. Read Exodus 15:6–12. How does this passage help you understand the references to God's right hand in Psalm 110:1 and 110:5?

2. Read Hebrews 1:1–14 and answer the following questions.

What common language and imagery do you notice between this passage and Psalm 110?

Who sits at God's right hand and why is this significant?

The author of Hebrews quotes Psalm 110 and draws a direct line to Christ as King and Lord. He also provides a full explanation of Melchizedek's significance, but before we take a look at that, let's see what the Old Testament says about this mysterious priest.

3. Melchizedek, the priest mentioned in Psalm 110:4, is only mentioned one other time in the Old Testament. Read Genesis 14:17–24 and answer the following questions.

Where is Melchizedek from?

What *two* positions does Melchizedek hold (v. 18)?

Melchizedek is the first priest mentioned in the Bible, but he is also said to be the king of Salem. New Testament scholar D. G. Peterson helpfully explains,

> Although Israelite kings sometimes exercised priestly functions, the distinction between the offices was much more definite in Israel than in neighbouring cultures. Psalm 110 therefore appears to be prophetic of a new situation in proclaiming that a Davidic king will be a priest forever according to the order of Melchizedek.[1]

So the reference to Melchizedek in Psalm 110 points to a future king who would also be a priest. To understand the significance of this, we first need to think about the office of priest in the Old Testament. The people of Israel consisted of twelve tribes, one of which was the tribe of Levi. According to Old Testament law, only Levites could serve as priests (Ex. 28:1; 29; Num. 3). Jesus, however, was not a descendant of Levi—he was a Davidic king (Luke 1:31–33), and David was from the tribe of Judah (Matt. 1:1–16).

4. Read Hebrews 5:1–10. How does this passage help you understand the reference to Melchizedek in Psalm 110:4?

5. Read Hebrews 7:1–3 and 7:15–17. How is Melchizedek like Jesus? How are Jesus and Melchizedek different from the Levitical priests?

---

1 Brian Rosner et al., eds., *New Dictionary of Biblical Theology: Exploring the Unity and Diversity of Scripture* (IVP Reference Collection, n.d.), 659.

Psalm 110 is a royal hymn that celebrates Christ Jesus, the Davidic king who sits at God's right hand. But Jesus is not just a king. He's also a priest. And unlike the former priests who offered bulls and goats, Jesus offered himself as the once-for-all sacrifice for sinners. The King who executes judgment stepped down from his throne to take our punishment upon himself. What other king would do this? What king would die for his people? Only Jesus—the King who will forever be a priest after the order of Melchizedek.

Application: How Do I Faithfully Respond?

6. Many view Jesus only as a baby in the manger, but Psalm 110 presents him as a King with a scepter who pours out his wrath on his enemies. How does this psalm correct or enhance your view of Jesus?

7. Jesus is the true King who deserves to reign over us. But if we're honest, we know we don't always submit to his leadership. In what ways do you sometimes allow other things (people, desires, habits, etc.) to rule and reign over you?

8. Psalm 110:3 says people will offer themselves to Christ on the day of his power. What would it look like for you to offer yourself to Jesus even now? What two or three things might you do to honor Christ as King of your life?

___

___

___

 Memory Verse

> Give the king your justice, O God,
>   and your righteousness to the royal son! (Ps. 72:1)

REFLECTION

When sharing the gospel, I've found it helpful to establish common ground by highlighting what's wrong with the world. All it takes is a reminder of the latest political controversy, fatal shooting, or devastating natural disaster and the person is immediately tracking with me. Some seem surprised when I say that this isn't the way life was supposed to be. Though we live amid great sin and suffering, humanity's first home was a place completely devoid of pain.

In the beginning, God created Adam and Eve, the first people, and put them in a beautiful garden in a place called Eden. The garden was "very good" as Scripture says, but it wasn't entirely safe. An enemy was present. Genesis explains that Satan, in the form of a serpent, sought to destroy the kingdom by introducing the idea of treason. And when Adam and Eve ate the forbidden fruit, everything changed. By disregarding the one command given, they essentially shook their fists at God and rejected his rule. So God did what any good king would do—he removed the kingdom threat. He sent Adam and Eve out of Eden, away from his presence, where life would never be the same. We call this the *fall of man*.

Fast forward a bit in the story, and you'll learn that God later chose a people for himself—the Israelites—and gave them a beautiful place to live too. Their situation should have been wonderful, but like Adam and Eve, the Israelites rejected God as King. The book of Judges reminds us that when Israel had no king, everyone did what was right in his own eyes. And the results were disastrous. We know this because we're still living it. The mottoes "You do you," "Live your truth," and "Follow your heart" are found everywhere from social media banners to cheap coffee mugs. The idea of obeying external authority figures has become passé. And the result of self-rule on a wide scale seems to bring anything but human flourishing.

Royal psalms like Psalm 72 remind us that we live in a broken world filled with sin and suffering, but they also lift our eyes to Jesus. He is the King who rules with perfect justice and righteousness. And he is the Priest who offered his own life to restore what we lost in the fall. He will return to establish his kingdom, and there won't be any enemies there. No one will commit treason. Everyone will love the King, and he will reign forever in a kingdom not bound by time.

Over the past few years, I've been thinking a lot about time. Perhaps this is what happens as we age. I often look back at old photos, wondering where the time went. I know the Bible says there is a time for everything and that dwelling on the past is futile, but something inside me wants to be in a place where good things never end.

The psalmists wanted eternal happiness too. They often prayed that a good king would live forever and maintain prosperity and blessing. But no king in history could guarantee lasting security. Only Jesus, the eternal King, can bring about an unending kingdom of righteousness, peace, and joy.

Royal psalms have become precious to me. They remind me that Christ will soon return and fully establish his good kingdom, where no one will be poor or oppressed and no one will do what is right in his own eyes. We will be his people, and he will be our God in a kingdom that far surpasses Eden because evil won't be there. So, on days when all we see is the darkness around us, royal psalms lift our eyes to the King who will reign in glory forever. Worship him. Pray for his return. Join the psalmist in song and lift your eyes to Jesus our King.

1. How do royal psalms help us think rightly about the future?

2. What part does hope play in your life when something unexpectedly difficult happens? Write the passages from Psalms 72 and 110 that would inspire you to turn your eyes to Christ in such times.

💙 **Memory Verse**

> Give the king your justice, O God,
>   and your righteousness to the royal son! (Ps. 72:1)

GROUP DISCUSSION QUESTIONS

Icebreaker: Share about a time when you met someone you really admired.

Warm-up: What are the most important qualities for a good leader to have?

1. What is the significance of the right hand of God? What does this image convey?

2. Royal psalms emphasize the importance of a ruler who will help the poor and needy. How does your understanding of Jesus's kingdom help you think rightly about social justice and oppression?

3. How do we know that Jesus's kingdom has not yet come in its fullness? What are some features of our current world that will be changed when Christ returns?

4. According to Old Testament law, only Levites could serve as priests. Jesus was from the tribe of Judah—not the tribe of Levi—so how can the author of Hebrews say Jesus is our "great high priest" (Heb. 4:14)? What role does Melchizedek play in your explanation?

5. Do you tend to think of Christ as a baby in a manger or a king who will one day judge his enemies? How does your view of Jesus affect your evangelism?

6. How do royal psalms find their ultimate fulfillment in Jesus?

7. What was one thing that convicted, encouraged, instructed, or stood out to you this week?

8. How did these psalms help you turn your eyes to Jesus?

What did you see or learn about Jesus?

What do you need to believe as a result?

How should you live differently?

♪ Hymn for the Week

"Hail to the Lord's Anointed"

Hail to the Lord's anointed
Great David's greater Son!
Hail in the time appointed,
His reign on earth begun!
He comes to break oppression,
To set the captive free;
To take away transgression,
And rule in equity.[2]

Additional Kingly Psalms for Further Study

Psalms 2, 18, 20, 21, 45, 89, 101, and 144

We've listed general questions in an appendix that you can use while studying these psalms.

---

2   James Montgomery, "Hail to the Lord's Annointed," 1821, https://hymnary.org.

Week 7

Turn to God in Trust

Psalms 27 and 16

The North Carolina mountains are home to America's highest suspension footbridge. Hanging at an elevation of 5,305 feet, it's known as the Mile High Swinging Bridge. Yes, you read that correctly—it swings. When I first saw it as a child, I hesitated to walk across. I was afraid of heights, and I wasn't sure I could trust this unstable looking structure to hold me up.

But when my parents stepped out and began walking across, my perspective changed. I didn't necessarily trust the bridge, but I did trust them. If they thought it was safe to cross, then I'd follow their lead.

In this week's psalms, we'll find David facing fears and dangers of his own. These psalms are called psalms of trust or confidence because they express trust in God amid shaky circumstances. Similar to how I found confidence to walk the bridge because I trusted my parents, David finds confidence to face enemies and threats because he trusts the Lord. When we place our trust in God, we can have confidence in the most uncertain times, knowing he will never fail us.

 Turn to God in Prayer

Father, when I face trouble and uncertainty it's easy to become fearful and anxious. Help me to trust in you, my light and my salvation (Ps. 27:1). Give me joy in your presence (Ps. 16:11) and help my heart to take courage as I wait on you (Ps. 27:14). In Jesus's name I pray, amen.

 Memory Verse

> The LORD is my light and my salvation;
>   whom shall I fear?
> The LORD is the stronghold of my life;
>   of whom shall I be afraid? (Ps. 27:1)

PSALM 27 OBSERVATION AND INTERPRETATION

Psalm 27

The LORD is My Light and My Salvation
Of David.

1 The LORD is my light and my salvation;
    whom shall I fear?
  The LORD is the stronghold of my life;
    of whom shall I be afraid?

2 When evildoers assail me
    to eat up my flesh,
  my adversaries and foes,
    it is they who stumble and fall.

3 Though an army encamp against me,
    my heart shall not fear;

though war arise against me,
 yet I will be confident.

4 One thing have I asked of the Lord,
  that will I seek after:
that I may dwell in the house of the Lord
 all the days of my life,
to gaze upon the beauty of the Lord
 and to inquire in his temple.

5 For he will hide me in his shelter
  in the day of trouble;
he will conceal me under the cover of his tent;
  he will lift me high upon a rock.

6 And now my head shall be lifted up
  above my enemies all around me,
and I will offer in his tent
  sacrifices with shouts of joy;
  I will sing and make melody to the Lord.

7 Hear, O Lord, when I cry aloud;
  be gracious to me and answer me!
8 You have said, "Seek my face."
My heart says to you,
  "Your face, Lord, do I seek."
9 Hide not your face from me.
Turn not your servant away in anger,
  O you who have been my help.
Cast me not off; forsake me not,
  O God of my salvation!

10 For my father and my mother have forsaken me,
   but the LORD will take me in.

11 Teach me your way, O LORD,
   and lead me on a level path
   because of my enemies.
12 Give me not up to the will of my adversaries;
   for false witnesses have risen against me,
   and they breathe out violence.

13 I believe that I shall look upon the goodness of the LORD
   in the land of the living!
14 Wait for the LORD;
   be strong, and let your heart take courage;
   wait for the LORD!

Imagine we're having lunch, and I'm unsure what to order. You've been to the restaurant before, so you recommend a dish and say, "You'll love it! Trust me." What would it look like for me to trust you in that situation? I'd order the dish. If I said, "I trust you," but ordered something else, my words wouldn't mean much. Trust is more than words—it's demonstrated by action.

Similarly, psalms of trust express truths about God and belief in his goodness. But they also describe actions that show us what it looks like to trust God. As we study Psalm 27 today, we'll begin to see that two important elements of trusting God are seeking and waiting.

Observation: What Does Psalm 27 Say?

Read Psalm 27 and answer the following questions.

TURN TO GOD IN TRUST   187

1. Based on verses 1–3 and 12, what sort of problem or fear does David seem to be facing?

2. What is David seeking in each of the following verses?

   Verse 4

   Verse 8

3. In verses 5–6, David repeats the phrases "he will" and "I will" to describe what God will do and how David will respond.

   What are three things God will do?

   How will David respond?

188 TURN TO GOD IN TRUST

4. In verses 13–14, David expresses his trust in God in terms of belief and action.

What does David believe (v. 13)?

What is David going to do (v. 14)?

When we face fear and uncertainty, we often rush to figure out what we can *do* about it. Maybe there's an expert we can call, a product we can buy, a plan we can put in place. And none of those things are necessarily bad—they may help address our circumstances. But as David shows us, the peace we crave in our souls is only found in the Lord. David is confident in the face of adversity not because of what *he* can do but because of what *God* can do.

Interpretation: What Does Psalm 27 Mean?

Remember chiastic structure? It's been a few weeks since we've considered it, but like some of our other psalms, Psalm 27 is organized by chiastic structure. It looks like this:[1]

Verse 1: Trust in God
    Verses 2–3: Danger from Enemies
        Verses 4–5: Seeking God
           Verse 6: Worship
        Verses 7–10: Seeking God
    Verses 11–12: Danger from Enemies
Verses 13–14: Trust in God

1   James M. Hamilton Jr., *Psalms: Volume I* (Lexham Academic, 2021), 327.

TURN TO GOD IN TRUST · 189

5. David expresses trust in God at the beginning and end of the psalm, but he does it in different ways.

In verse 1, David expresses trust in God's character and work. What do you think David wants to convey about God by each of these descriptions?

My light

My salvation

The stronghold of my life

6. David ends the psalm with an encouragement to wait on God. How might waiting on God be an expression of trust?

7. In verse 4, David says he has asked the Lord for "one thing," but then he lists several things. Reread the two sections about seeking God (vv. 4–5 and 7–10). What do you think David means when he says there's "one thing" he will seek after?

8. As we've learned, the focus of chiastic structure is the middle. So in this case verse 6 is the focus where David describes worshiping God. How do you think trust and worship are related?

We learn something about trust as we consider the psalm's structure. Biblical trust isn't pretending everything is fine. It's not ignoring or refusing to think about our problems. David is realistic about the trouble he's facing and devotes two sections to describing it.

Biblical trust is active. It remembers God's character and promises, seeks God's presence, and waits on God's provision. And as we see at the center of the chiasm, trust ultimately overflows into worship. If you're facing uncertainty or adversity today, don't ignore it. Like David, consider your circumstances in light of who God is. Seek God's presence and let your heart turn from worry to worship.

💙 Memory Verse

> The LORD is my light and my salvation;
>   whom shall I fear?
> The LORD is the stronghold of my life;
>   of whom shall I be afraid? (Ps. 27:1)

PSALM 27 INTERPRETATION AND APPLICATION

Some people are good at casting vision and big ideas. I'm not one of them. I'm the super practical, detail-oriented person always saying, "That sounds great! But how will we *do* it?" And I often have a similar question as I read the Bible. When I read verses about seeking God or waiting on the Lord, I want to do it, but I'm not always sure what it looks like.

So today we're going to get a little more practical. We'll explore verses from other parts of the Bible that help us understand what it means to seek and wait. And we'll consider how to apply those ideas in our lives.

Interpretation: What Does the Whole Bible Say?

Read Psalm 27 and answer the following questions.

1. As David opens Psalm 27, he answers his fear by remembering God's character and work. In Romans 8, Paul writes in a similar way and shows that our ultimate comfort is found in the work of Christ. Read Romans 8:31–32. How does looking to Christ's death on the cross give us confidence to trust God no matter our circumstances?

2. In Psalm 27, David seeks God's presence and face. Read the passages below. How does each one help us understand what it might look like to seek God?

Matthew 7:7-11

Psalm 119:10

3. David ends the psalm with an encouragement to "wait for the LORD" (v. 14). Read the verses below. How does each one help us understand what it means to wait on God?

Psalm 37:34

Psalm 130:5

Proverbs 20:22

Did you notice that seeking and waiting have something in common? Both involve obedience—keeping God's commandments and walking in his ways. It can be tempting to take matters into our own hands when we encounter dif-

Application: How Do I Faithfully Respond?

4. What do you tend to seek when you face trouble or uncertainty—physical comfort, answers and solutions, distractions, etc.? What might it look like for you to seek God's presence instead?

5. What's a situation in your life where you're navigating uncertainty or adversity? How can you walk in obedience as you wait on the Lord?

6. In a devotion about Psalm 27, Tim Keller wrote, "Our fears can serve an important purpose—they show us where we have really located our heart's treasure. Follow the pathway of fear back into your heart to discover the things you love more than God."[2]

---

ficulty or uncertainty, especially when God seems slow to answer. We might be tempted to disregard biblical wisdom or excuse sin to get the results we want. But God calls us to wait on him. And we can be sure he's not holding out on us. He gave us the very best thing when he sent Jesus to die on the cross for our sins, and he will not withhold anything that's for our good.

---

2 Timothy Keller and Kathy Keller, *The Songs of Jesus: A Year of Daily Devotions in the Psalms* (Viking, 2015), 50.

What are some things you fear?

What might your fears reveal about who or what you love most?

7. In Psalm 27:5, David describes how God will help him "in the day of trouble." David doesn't expect that trouble will never come but that God will take care of him when it does. If the things you fear happen, how do you think God will care for you?

One of the most beautiful truths of Scripture is that God not only invites us to seek him but he sent Jesus to seek us. Jesus says in Luke 19:10 that he came "to seek and to save the lost." Are you struggling with fear and uncertainty today? Take heart and trust the Lord. Seek the Savior who came to seek you.

💙 Memory Verse

> The LORD is my light and my salvation;
>   whom shall I fear?
> The LORD is the stronghold of my life;
>   of whom shall I be afraid? (Ps. 27:1)

PSALM 16 OBSERVATION AND INTERPRETATION

Psalm 16

You Will Not Abandon My Soul
A Miktam of David.

¹ Preserve me, O God, for in you I take
    refuge.
² I say to the Lord, "You are my Lord;
    I have no good apart from you."

³ As for the saints in the land, they are
    the excellent ones,
  in whom is all my delight.

⁴ The sorrows of those who run after
    another god shall multiply;
  their drink offerings of blood I will
    not pour out
  or take their names on my lips.

⁵ The Lord is my chosen portion and
    my cup;
  you hold my lot.
⁶ The lines have fallen for me in pleasant
    places;
  indeed, I have a beautiful inheritance.

⁷ I bless the Lord who gives me counsel;
  in the night also my heart
    instructs me.
⁸ I have set the Lord always before me;
  because he is at my right hand, I shall
    not be shaken.

TURN TO GOD IN TRUST

⁹ Therefore my heart is glad, and my whole being rejoices;
    my flesh also dwells secure.
¹⁰ For you will not abandon my soul to Sheol,
    or let your holy one see corruption.

¹¹ You make known to me the path of life;
    in your presence there is fullness of joy;
    at your right hand are pleasures forevermore.

I'm an avid reader and former English teacher with what many people would consider a very bad habit—I almost always read the end of a novel first. I know I'm supposedly spoiling the story, but I think it enables me to enjoy the book more. When I don't know how a story ends, I race through the pages, trying to resolve the tension as quickly as possible. But when I know the end, I can slow down and appreciate the twists and turns along the way.

Today as we turn to Psalm 16, we'll find a similar dynamic at play. In this psalm of trust, David expresses great joy amid difficulty because he knows how his story will ultimately end.

Observation: What Does Psalm 16 Say?

Read Psalm 16 and answer the following questions.

1. In verse 1, which words suggest David is facing trouble?

TURN TO GOD IN TRUST   197

2. According to verse 4, what causes sorrows to multiply?

3. Read verses 2, 5, and 6. Where does David's "good" come from?

4. What gives David joy or delight according to each of the following verses?

Verse 3

Verses 8–9

Verse 11

In Psalm 27, David talked a lot about his trouble, but in Psalm 16 he only hints at it, devoting most of the psalm to explaining why he has joy amid trouble. As Dr. James Hamilton explains in his commentary on this psalm,

> To gain [God] is to gain the one who made and controls everything, inventor of every pleasure, insurer of all safety, definer of right and wrong, and rewarder of those who seek him. To lose him, even if you gained the world in exchange, would be to lose everything. . . . Anyone seeking pleasure, joy, satisfaction, and happiness should seek [the Lord].[3]

Let's take a closer look at some verses in this psalm that will help us understand how David seeks God and finds joy in him.

Interpretation: What Does Psalm 16 Mean?

5. In verse 3, David says he delights in "the saints," in other words, God's people. Why might other believers be a source of delight for David?

6. In verses 5–6, David uses imagery of land and territory when he talks about his "lot" and how the "lines have fallen for [him] in pleasant places." Land was significant in Old Testament times because it related to social standing and reputation, material wealth and prosperity, inheritance and future security for a family.[4] What do you think David wants to convey with this land imagery? What might he mean when he says the Lord is his "portion"?

---

3 Hamilton, *Psalms Volume I*, 215.
4 Hamilton, *Psalms Volume I*, 215.

7. In verse 8, David describes God's presence with him using two different images: the Lord being *before him* and the Lord being *beside him* ("at his right hand").

What do you think it means for God to be *before* David? How does it help to have someone go ahead of you?

What do you think it means for God to be *beside* David? How does it help to have someone by your side?

8. In verse 11, David mentions the right hand again, but he says there are "pleasures forevermore" at *God's* right hand. What do you think it means for a person to be at God's right hand?

God is at David's right hand—walking beside him as his constant companion and help, upholding him so he will "not be shaken" (v. 8). And David anticipates that one day he will be at God's right hand in heaven where there are pleasures forevermore. David faces trouble and uncertainty with confidence because he knows he's not alone—God is with him. And he knows his current trouble isn't the end of the story. However long he may endure hardship now, he will experience the joy of God's presence for eternity. That's how the story ends for David and for all who are in Christ. We too can have joy amid trouble as we remember these truths—God is with us now and we will be with him forever!

💙 Memory Verse

> The LORD is my light and my salvation;
>   whom shall I fear?
> The LORD is the stronghold of my life;
>   of whom shall I be afraid? (Ps. 27:1)

PSALM 16 INTERPRETATION AND APPLICATION

When we say someone is living "the good life," we usually intend to paint a picture of wealth and ease. We might imagine someone who takes luxurious vacations, lives in a beautiful home, and has all the conveniences money can buy. We tend to think of our good in terms of wealth and material possessions.

But that's not what David has in mind in Psalm 16. When he talks about his good, his portion, and his inheritance, David is talking about the Lord. Today we'll look to some other passages of Scripture to help us understand David's idea of "the good life."

Interpretation: What Does the Whole Bible Say?

Read Psalm 16 and answer the following questions.

1. In verse 2, David says to God, "I have no good apart from you." How do each of the verses below help you understand what David means?

   Philippians 3:8

   James 1:17

2. In verses 5–6, David expresses trust in God, rather than material wealth, as his security and provision. Read Matthew 6:25–33.

   Why should we trust God to provide for our needs?

   What might it mean to seek God's kingdom and righteousness first?

3. In verse 6, David says he has "a beautiful inheritance." Read 1 Peter 1:3–5. What do you think it means to have an inheritance in Christ?

4. In Acts 2, the apostle Peter quoted Psalm 16:8–11 in a sermon. He explained that these verses are not just about David; they point forward to Jesus.

Read John 14:1–6. How did God "make known to [us] the path of life" (Ps. 16:11) in Jesus?

Read John 16:20–22. How is "fullness of joy" (Ps. 16:11) found in Christ?

Acts 2 records that the people listening to Peter's sermon were "cut to the heart" (v. 37) and asked him what they should do in response. Peter said, "Repent and be baptized every one of you in the name of Jesus Christ for the forgiveness of your sins" (v. 38). The good, joyful life David describes in Psalm 16 is only found in relationship with God through Jesus Christ. If you've never repented of your sin and put your trust in Christ for salvation, that's the most important way you can apply this passage. If you already have faith in Christ, let's consider how this psalm can help you grow in trusting God.

Application: How Do I Faithfully Respond?

5. In verse 2, when David says to God, "You are my Lord," the Hebrew word he uses means "master." David is saying God is the one who orders his life and directs what he should do.[5] In other words, God is in charge, and David trusts that submitting to God is for his good.

What's an area of your life where you struggle to obey God?

How would submitting to God in this area be good for you?

6. In verse 4, David talks about the sorrows of people who "run after another god." We don't worship idols in the same way as people in David's time, but we may worship things like money, control, comfort, health, and beauty. What "other gods" are you tempted to run after? What kinds of sorrows have you experienced from seeking those things rather than the Lord?

---

5 James Montgomery Boice, *Psalms: Volume 1* (Baker, 1994), 132.

7. David finds joy by remembering God's presence with him now and looking forward to being in God's presence for eternity.

What are some ways you sense God's presence in your life or see him upholding you now?

_____

_____

What could you do this week to help you look forward to the joy of being in God's presence forever?

_____

_____

By the time we reach the end of Psalm 16, we could almost forget David is writing in a time of trouble because he devotes so much of the psalm to his joy. But where he ends has a lot to do with where he begins. He doesn't come to the Lord kicking and screaming, demanding a change of circumstances. He comes in submission saying, *You're in charge, Lord. You know what's best. And if I have you, I have all I need.*

We tend to think joy comes on the other side of trouble, but David shows us we can have joy amid trouble when we trust the Lord. If you're in Christ, God is with you now, and you will be with him forever. Though everything else in your life might be cause for sorrow, that's cause for joy!

💙 Memory Verse

> The LORD is my light and my salvation;
>   whom shall I fear?
> The LORD is the stronghold of my life;
>   of whom shall I be afraid? (Ps. 27:1)

REFLECTION

When my grandfather left for Europe to serve in World War II, I can only imagine how worried his mother must have been. As a mom of three sons, the thought of sending my boys off to war is agonizing. I never met my great-grandmother, so I don't know what she felt as she waited and wondered if he would come home. But I do know what she did.

She prayed Psalm 121. It's a beautiful psalm of trust that opens with the psalmist asking himself a simple but important question: "From where does my help come?" (v. 1). He declares, "My help comes from the LORD" (v. 2) and goes on to describe God as our "keeper" who never slumbers or sleeps (v. 4). He continues,

> The LORD will keep you from all evil;
>   he will keep your life.
> The LORD will keep
>   your going out and your coming in
>   from this time forth and forevermore. (Ps. 121:7–8)

My great-grandmother prayed Psalm 121 every day my grandfather was gone during the war. And unbeknownst to her, she set an example for generations of parents in our family to pray this psalm for their children. I pray it regularly for my sons, her great-great-grandchildren.

For a long time, I've thought of this practice primarily as a neat tradition. But as I studied and wrote about Psalms 27 and 16, it occurred to me that my great-grandmother did much more than start a tradition—she taught generations what it looks like to trust God. As we've talked about this week, trust isn't just about what we say or feel or think—it's demonstrated by what we do.

When we encounter trouble and uncertainty, the place we turn for help says a lot about who or what we trust. If we let our actions answer the psalmist's question—"From where does my help come?"—what would we find? Perhaps our help comes from Google, or social media influencers, or money, or our own efforts. Perhaps we think if we just work hard enough or get the right people on our side or do enough research, we'll get the outcome we want.

But when you send a son off to war, it's pretty clear there's nothing you can do to ensure he comes back home. Those sorts of situations make us see what's actually true in every situation—"My help comes from the LORD" (Ps. 121:2).

Whatever difficulty or uncertainty you're facing today, turn to God in trust. Seek him in his word and in prayer. As my great-grandmother reminds us, psalms aren't just meant to be read and studied—they're meant to be prayed! Pray one of the psalms of trust we studied this week, or pray Psalm 121.

Since I'm here to tell the story, you probably guessed that my grandfather returned from the war safe and sound. But even if the outcome had been different, my great-grandmother's prayers would not have been in vain. Each time she opened her Bible to Psalm 121, she didn't just find a template for her prayers, she found truths to comfort her soul. When we trust the Lord, we won't always get the results we want. But we will find rest in the one we truly need.

1. How can the psalms of trust help us seek and wait on the Lord when we face trouble?

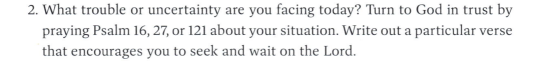

2. What trouble or uncertainty are you facing today? Turn to God in trust by praying Psalm 16, 27, or 121 about your situation. Write out a particular verse that encourages you to seek and wait on the Lord.

💙 Memory Verse

> The LORD is my light and my salvation;
>   whom shall I fear?
> The LORD is the stronghold of my life;
>   of whom shall I be afraid? (Ps. 27:1)

GROUP DISCUSSION QUESTIONS

Icebreaker: What's one of your irrational fears?

Warm-up: What do you think makes someone trustworthy?

1. David was seeking "one thing"—to dwell in the Lord's presence—but we live in a culture that's seeking "all the things." How can we seek the Lord's presence in our lives amid all the hustle and hurry?

2. What difference does it make to understand that trust is demonstrated by what we do not just by what we say or feel?

3. How can psalms of trust help us move from worry to worship?

4. How do seeking the Lord, waiting on the Lord, and obeying the Lord each demonstrate trust in him?

5. What are some "other gods" you're tempted to trust in? Why does running after other gods lead to sorrow?

6. What difference does it make in our trouble and uncertainty if we understand like David that our "good" and our "portion" are ultimately found in the Lord?

7. What was one thing that convicted, encouraged, instructed, or stood out to you this week?

8. How did these psalms help you turn your eyes to Jesus?

What did you see or learn about Jesus?

What do you need to believe as a result?

How should you live differently?

♪ Hymn for the Week

"'Tis So Sweet to Trust in Jesus"

I'm so glad I learned to trust Him,
Precious Jesus, Savior, Friend:
And I know that He is with me,
Will be with me to the end.

Jesus, Jesus, how I trust Him!
How I've proved Him o'er and o'er!
Jesus, Jesus, precious Jesus!
Oh, for grace to trust Him more![6]

---

6 Louisa M. R. Stead, "'Tis So Sweet to Trust in Jesus," 1882, https://hymnary.org.

Additional Psalms of Trust for Further Study

Psalms 23, 62, 73, 91, 115, 125, and 131

We've listed general questions in an appendix that you can use while studying these psalms.

Week 8

Turn to God in Praise

Psalms 46 and 84

In the summer of 1886, Swedish pastor Carl Boberg was caught in a terrible thunderstorm. But when the booming thunder and flashes of lightning finally stopped, something surprising happened. The sky cleared, and Boberg heard birds singing in the trees. The glory of creation was on full display. Boberg responded by penning "How Great Thou Art," a beautiful nine-stanza hymn of praise. The song's repeated refrain captures his response to God's amazing power:

> Then sings my soul, my Savior God, to Thee,
> How great Thou art, how great Thou art![1]

More than a century later, this beautiful hymn is still cherished by Christians and sung in churches around the world.

---

1 Carl Boberg, "How Great Thou Art," trans. Stuart K. Hine, 1949, https://hymnary.org. © Hope Publishing.

In this final week of our study, we turn to psalms of praise. Just as Boberg's experience with the majesty of creation left him in awe of God, the psalmists' meditation on God's attributes and deeds led them to write songs inviting all people to praise God. Praise psalms call us to admire God for who he is, deepen our sense of reverence and awe as we consider his majesty, and give us language to express the joy he has placed in our hearts. Not only will our souls sing when we read praise psalms, but so will our voices.

 Turn to God in Prayer

Father God, you are worthy of all worship, honor, and praise. Open my eyes to see you as I study, and help me to praise you with everything that is within me (Ps. 150:6). In Jesus's name I pray, amen.

Memory Verse

> Blessed are those who dwell in your house,
> ever singing your praise! (Ps. 84:4)

PSALM 46 OBSERVATION AND INTERPRETATION

Psalm 46

God Is Our Fortress
To the choirmaster. Of the Sons of Korah. According to Alamoth. A Song.

> ¹ God is our refuge and strength,
>   a very present help in trouble.
> ² Therefore we will not fear though the
>   earth gives way,
>   though the mountains be moved into
>   the heart of the sea,
> ³ though its waters roar and foam,
>   though the mountains tremble at its
>   swelling. *Selah*

4 There is a river whose streams make glad the city of God,
    the holy habitation of the Most High.
5 God is in the midst of her; she shall not be moved;
    God will help her when morning dawns.
6 The nations rage, the kingdoms totter;
    he utters his voice, the earth melts.
7 The LORD of hosts is with us;
    the God of Jacob is our fortress. *Selah*

8 Come, behold the works of the LORD,
    how he has brought desolations on the earth.
9 He makes wars cease to the end of the earth;
    he breaks the bow and shatters the spear;
    he burns the chariots with fire.
10 "Be still, and know that I am God.
    I will be exalted among the nations,
    I will be exalted in the earth!"
11 The LORD of hosts is with us;
    the God of Jacob is our fortress. *Selah*

A friend of mine stopped watching the evening news because she said it made her anxious. She just didn't want to know about every frightening thing happening in the world. I totally get it. While headlines keep us informed, they also remind us of the constant threat of devastating natural disasters, destructive wars, and all sorts of imminent danger. I still watch the news, but sometimes it makes me want to find a place to hide.

Our first psalm this week recognizes the present trouble facing the world and uses it as a backdrop for God's glory. As we learn about his care for us when chaos and danger abound, our hearts will be filled with gratitude and our mouths with praise.

TURN TO GOD IN PRAISE

Observation: What Does Psalm 46 Say?

1. This psalm uses imagery, hyperbole, and contrast. Use the following questions to make observations about each of these important literary devices.

   Imagery: To what important structure is God compared in verses 1, 7, and 11?

   Hyperbole: Hyperbole is a literary device in which exaggeration is used to elicit a particular response. In verses 2–3, what does the psalmist say might happen to the mountains? To the earth's waters?

   Contrast: What is moved in verse 2? What will *not* be moved according to verses 4–5?

2. How is the "city of God" described in verses 4–5? Who resides there?

3. In verse 6, what is happening on earth? What happens when God speaks?

4. An imperative in Scripture is a command or request. List the two imperatives given in verses 8–10.

a.

b.

The psalmist invites us to recognize God's power and to rest in his sovereign control. In light of who God is, we should be still and acknowledge his power and glory.

Interpretation: What Does Psalm 46 Mean?

5. Read Psalm 46:1–3 and answer the following questions.

How does the imagery in verse 1 work together with the imagery of verses 2–3 to emphasize God's care for his people?

Based on these first three verses of the psalm, why is God worthy of praise?

6. Read verses 4–7 again. Although the mountains are moved into the heart of the sea (v. 2), the city of God shall not be moved (v. 5). According to verse 5, what explains the city's success? Why would this be a reason to praise God?

7. The earth is described in verse 6 with a term the Old Testament uses to describe the Canaanites' response to God's people (Ex. 15:15). Why do you think the earth melts when God speaks?

In the first seven verses of Psalm 46, the author provides many reasons to view God as our refuge and help in times of trouble. Then in verses 8–10, the reader is called to respond. First, the psalmist calls the reader to "Come, behold the works of the LORD," then God calls the reader to "Be still, and know" that he is God.

8. How do these two imperatives work together to teach the reader how to respond to God's acts? What does this teach us about the author's purpose in writing the psalm?

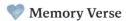

The phrase "Be still" in verse 10 has less to do with quiet meditation than it does with awestruck surrender.[2] While chaos may exist on earth, God is in control and his people are safe in his midst. The God of Jacob is our fortress.

💙 Memory Verse

> Blessed are those who dwell in your house,
>   ever singing your praise! (Ps. 84:4)

PSALM 46 INTERPRETATION AND APPLICATION

If you took a poll asking people how they think the world will end, you'd likely hear all sorts of guesses. Some believe global warming will eventually make the earth uninhabitable. Some believe nuclear war will be our doom. But the Bible teaches that the world will end with the judgment of God.

Whether or not the author knew it, Psalm 46 points forward to the day of God's final judgment. Today, let's look at some passages that help us better interpret the psalm so we can apply it to our lives.

Interpretation: What Does the Whole Bible Say?

1. Some of the imagery in Psalm 46 is similar to the judgment language found in Revelation, the final book of the Bible. Read Revelation 6:12–17 and answer the following questions.

---

2 Christopher Ash, *Teaching Psalms Volume Two: From Text to Message*, rev. ed. (Christian Focus, 2018), 107.

What similar imagery do you notice between Revelation 6:12–17 and Psalm 46:1–3?

Read Hebrews 9:27 and John 5:21–24. How can we survive God's coming judgment?

2. In some translations, Psalm 16:8 reads, "I have set the LORD always before me; / because he is at my right hand, I shall not be *shaken*." How does this help you understand Psalm 46:4–7? Why is the psalmist not *shaken* or *moved*?

3. Throughout the Old Testament, Zion represents the place of God's presence and is sometimes referred to as the "city of God" (2 Sam. 5:1–7; Pss. 2:6; 48:1–3; 76:1–2; 87:1–2). In Revelation, we learn about a new city of God. Read Revelation 22:1–5.

   How does this passage relate to Psalm 46:4–7? What do you think is the connection between these two cities (see Rev. 3:12; Heb. 11:13–16)?

According to Revelation 22:3, who will dwell with God and the Lamb in the beautiful city?

4. The crossing of the Red Sea is one of the most pivotal events recorded in Scripture (Ex. 14:1–31) and is in the background of many psalms. Consider the significance of the Red Sea crossing as you answer the following questions.

Read Psalm 66:1–7 and explain how this passage helps you understand the imperatives in Psalm 46:8.

Read Exodus 14:1–13. How do Moses's instructions help you understand the imperatives found in Psalm 46:10?

In Revelation 6:15–16, we learn some will try to hide from God on judgment day. But Jesus said those who trust in him will have no need to hide (John 5:24). Instead of coming into judgment, they will enter eternal life. What better reason do we need to praise God?

Application: How Do I Faithfully Respond?

5. When we look around at the trouble in our world, it's tempting to seek a way of escape. Where do you turn when there is difficulty or danger in your life?

What could you do to turn to God as your refuge when the world's chaos overwhelms you?

6. Psalm 46 points forward to a day when creation will unravel and safety will only be found in God. How does trusting in Christ help you anticipate this day with confidence rather than fear? How does this psalm motivate you to share the salvation message with others?

7. Sometimes the troubles of life make it hard to praise God, but psalms of praise can reorient our hearts and cultivate joy. What makes it hard for you to praise God? How has Psalm 46 encouraged you to admire and celebrate God despite those challenges?

8. The Israelites could stand in silence and stillness because God promised to fight for them. What would it look like for you to be still even amid life's troubles?

God is our help in life now, but more importantly, he will be our help when he judges the world. On that day, Christ will be our safe place. New Testament scholar Tom Schreiner writes of God's future judgment, "The saints sing because they are saved, while their enemies are judged. Believers are full of praise for the new exodus, the climactic act of redemption accomplished by Jesus Christ."[3] If you are in Christ, you have a reason to praise the Lord. God is our refuge, strength, and mighty fortress. Let's exalt his name together!

Memory Verse

> Blessed are those who dwell in your house,
> ever singing your praise! (Ps. 84:4)

PSALM 84 OBSERVATION AND INTERPRETATION

Psalm 84

My Soul Longs for the Courts of the LORD
To the choirmaster: according to The Gittith. A Psalm of the Sons of Korah.

> 1 How lovely is your dwelling place,
>   O LORD of hosts!
> 2 My soul longs, yes, faints
>   for the courts of the LORD;

---

3 Thomas R. Schreiner, "Revelation," in *ESV Expository Commentary: Hebrews–Revelation* (Crossway, 2018), 684.

my heart and flesh sing for joy
    to the living God.

3 Even the sparrow finds a home,
    and the swallow a nest for herself,
    where she may lay her young,
at your altars, O LORD of hosts,
    my King and my God.
4 Blessed are those who dwell in your house,
    ever singing your praise! *Selah*

5 Blessed are those whose strength is in you,
    in whose heart are the highways to Zion.
6 As they go through the Valley of Baca
    they make it a place of springs;
    the early rain also covers it with pools.
7 They go from strength to strength;
    each one appears before God in Zion.

8 O LORD God of hosts, hear my prayer;
    give ear, O God of Jacob! *Selah*
9 Behold our shield, O God;
    look on the face of your anointed!

10 For a day in your courts is better
    than a thousand elsewhere.
I would rather be a doorkeeper in the house of my God
    than dwell in the tents of wickedness.
11 For the LORD God is a sun and shield;
    the LORD bestows favor and honor.
No good thing does he withhold
    from those who walk uprightly.

¹² O Lord of hosts,
blessed is the one who trusts in you!

The campus of Southern Seminary in Louisville, Kentucky, is one of my favorite places on earth. I was an online student, but I took a number of classes that included a few days on campus. I loved everything about being there—the huge courtyard filled with trees and surrounded by red brick buildings; the snapshots on the wall of former students, many of whom have authored some of the most respected theological resources available; and the coffee shop where I enjoyed eavesdropping on theological debates among the next generation of biblical scholars. Each time I left Southern Seminary, my heart was full, and I couldn't wait until my next trip back.

Puritan preacher Jonathan Edwards once said in a sermon, "God is the highest good of the reasonable creature, and the enjoyment of him is the only happiness with which our souls can be satisfied. To go to heaven fully to enjoy God, is infinitely better than the most pleasant accommodations here."[4] As we turn to Psalm 84 today, we will see that no favorite place—not even a beautiful seminary campus—compares to the presence of the living God.

Observation: What Does Psalm 84 Say?

Read Psalm 84 and answer the following questions.

1. What does the psalmist desire according to verses 1–2? According to verse 10?

---

4   Jonathan Edwards, "The Christian Pilgrim, Section II," in *92 Sermons by Jonathan Edwards* (Monergism, 2017), https://www.monergism.com.

TURN TO GOD IN PRAISE

2. Where are the people in verses 5–7 going? What repeated word expresses what they need to get to this place?

3. How are the "blessed" described in each of the following verses?

Verse 4

Verse 5

Verse 12

4. According to verse 11, what will God do for those who walk uprightly?

Like Psalm 46, this psalm mentions Zion as the place where God dwells (v. 7). The author calls God's dwelling place his "courts," his "altars," and his "house." Let's take a closer look to better understand why there are so many references to the place of God's presence.

Interpretation: What Does Psalm 84 Mean?

5. For each passage given in the chart below, explain how the psalmist uses the type of figurative language listed to help you understand his longing to be in God's dwelling place.

Psalm 84 Verses	Figurative Language
1–2	Hyperbole:
3–4	Imagery:
5–7	Imagery:
10–12	Contrast:

6. The Hebrew word translated "blessed" in this Psalm (vv. 4, 5, and 12) is the same word found in Psalm 1:1. It describes one who is "happy" in God. But this happiness is not a fleeting or circumstantial happiness. It is grounded in a covenant relationship with the Lord and results in a deep sense of peace and delight. In this psalm, the "blessed" ones dwell in God's house, singing his praises; they find their strength in God; and they trust in God. Why do you think the psalmist links these behaviors with happiness in God?

7. Not much is known about the Valley of Baca, but verse 6 suggests it is a dry, hard place. According to verses 5–7, why might the people traveling to Zion need strength to get there? Where do they find this strength?

8. What do you think the psalmist means when he writes in verse 11 that God withholds no good thing from those who walk uprightly? How might meditating on this truth help those who lack joy?

Praise psalms are similar to thanksgiving psalms. Both declare God's goodness. But praise psalms emphasize who God *is* over what God *has done*. They often celebrate the wonder of simply being in God's presence. The author of Psalm 84 wants nothing more than to be in Zion, at the house of the Lord, singing God's praises with God's people. He knows that the nearness of God is his ultimate good. Take a moment to reflect on what this psalm has already taught us. Can you imagine anything better than a day with the King?

 **Memory Verse**

> Blessed are those who dwell in your house,
>   ever singing your praise! (Ps. 84:4)

PSALM 84 INTERPRETATION AND APPLICATION

Zion is the key to understanding Psalm 84. It was the Old Testament city of Jerusalem (2 Sam. 5:6–7) where the temple stood (2 Chron. 3:1) on Mount Moriah. The Israelites would journey to Zion for pilgrimage festivals that included animal sacrifices, teaching, and worship. But the temple was destroyed in 587 BC, so how could this psalm possibly apply to us? Today, let's consider other Bible passages that will help us discover the wonderful and exciting meaning of this psalm of praise.

Interpretation: What Does the Whole Bible Say?

1. The Old Testament temple was a fixed structure in Zion, but something changed when Jesus came to earth. According to the following New Testament verses, how did God's dwelling with his people change?

John 1:14

John 2:18–22

Matthew 12:1–6

2. Before the resurrected Christ ascended to heaven, he promised that the Holy Spirit would live in his followers (Acts 1:1–8). According to these passages, where is the temple now?

1 Corinthians 3:16

1 Peter 2:4–5

Ephesians 2:19–22

3. In Psalm 84:5–7, the author describes Zion as the ultimate destination for God's people. Read Hebrews 12:18–24 and answer these questions about Zion.

What is "the heavenly Jerusalem" (Heb. 12:22)?

Who will live there?

How does this help you understand Psalm 84?

The temple in Zion pointed forward to Jesus who said *he* was the true temple. The local church, as the gathering of God's people on earth, is the present-day "temple" and foreshadows the new Jerusalem that will come down from heaven

(Heb. 12:22). In that place, the Lord will be our temple (Rev. 21:22). And we, like this psalmist, will sing praises to our king forever (22:3).

Application: How Do I Faithfully Respond?

4. The author of Psalm 84 wants nothing more than to be with God.

What are some things you tend to desire more than time with God?

How might singing this psalm cultivate a deeper longing for God's presence in your life?

5. The Bible teaches that life is like a journey to God (1 Pet. 1:18–21; Heb. 13:14–15), but it's easy to get so wrapped up in our circumstances so we forget this earth is not our forever home. What might it look like for you to keep eternity in mind despite your circumstances? How might this bring you greater joy?

6. In verse 4, the psalmist looks forward to being with God's people, singing his praises. The gathering of the local church is a foretaste of corporate worship in heaven. Based on Psalm 84, how should we feel about the local church?

What two or three things can you do to deepen your relationships with others in your church?

7. The final verse of Psalm 84 reminds us that only the upright will receive good from God. On our own we cannot walk uprightly (Rom. 3:23), but Christ lived a perfect life in our place.

Have you put your trust in Christ, or are you trusting in your own ability to live a good life? How does Psalm 84 motivate you to follow Jesus more closely?

What good gifts has God given you in Christ? How does this motivate you to praise the Lord?

Have you ever heard the old adage "Some people are so heavenly minded that they're no earthly good?" I think the author of Psalm 84 would disagree. In fact, he would probably tell us to spend *more* time thinking about eternity. This doesn't mean we should live in denial of life's challenges. But we should allow our troubles to deepen our longing for home and fuel our praise for the God who has lovingly given our pain an expiration date. I love the way Old

Testament scholar Christopher Ash explains this: "We praise, not because the present is easy, but because the future is glorious."[5]

💙 Memory Verse

> Blessed are those who dwell in your house,
>   ever singing your praise! (Ps. 84:4)

REFLECTION

I absolutely love singing. My husband knows exactly what to expect if he walks into our bathroom while I'm getting ready for church on a Sunday morning—a full-volume worship band practice between me and my phone. I come from a long line of worshipers. My grandpa was a deacon who sang in his church choir, and my aunt Candy has the voice of an angel. She brought me to tears when she sang "The 23rd Psalm" during our wedding ceremony. In college, I sang in a Christian acapella group, and for years I've served on praise teams at church. Maybe that's why praise psalms are my favorite.

While psalms of lament give language to our sorrows and psalms of thanksgiving aid us in expressing gratitude, praise psalms serve a different purpose altogether. They are designed for pure joy! They are the psalms we sing when we just want to tell God how amazing he is and how much we love being in his presence as his children.

Even though I've been told that I have a joyful countenance, I went through a season of feeling so depressed that I didn't want to get out of bed in the morn-

---

5   Christopher Ash, *Teaching Psalms Volume One: From Text to Message* (Christian Focus, 2021), 209.

ing. On many Sundays, I wiped tears off my cheeks just before walking onstage to sing. I wonder if anyone in the congregation knew how much I needed to see and hear them praising God during those dark days. Their voices reminded me that my pain would not be wasted, my sorrow wouldn't last forever, and no matter how many things had been taken from me, I still had what I needed most because I still had Christ. I had salvation!

Ever since the events of Genesis 3, humanity has needed to get back to God's presence, and Christ, the Son of God incarnate, has accomplished this for us through his life, death, and resurrection. By singing the praise psalms, we cultivate delight in our salvation. This delight forms us into the kind of people who love God and who when tempted to sin, quickly realize it's not worth it. We sing not in the absence of sorrow but in spite of it.

Praise psalms remind us that even if God never grants us one more good gift, he is still worthy of extravagant praise and worship simply because of who he is. These beautiful songs are filled with doctrine. Through them we learn about God's nature and attributes, which show us how worthy he is of praise. These psalms captivate our hearts as we consider that the God of the universe desires to dwell with us and that through Christ he has made a way for that to happen. We need praise psalms because they celebrate the wonder of God's love and shape us into people who would trade a thousand days on earth to sit at God's feet for one night.

1. How do praise psalms help us remember our joy in Christ?

2. How did Psalm 46 and Psalm 84 turn your eyes to Jesus this week?

___

___

___

💙 **Memory Verse**

> Blessed are those who dwell in your house,
> ever singing your praises! (Ps. 84:4)

GROUP DISCUSSION QUESTIONS

Icebreaker: What is something that has brought you joy in the past week?

Warm-up: Why do you think praise and worship are usually mentioned as a pair?

1. Praise is an expression of admiration. How do praise psalms motivate us to express admiration to God?

___

___

___

2. Praise psalms are honest about life's troubles but turn our eyes to God and the help he provides. Where are you tempted to turn for help when life is

hard? How might remembering that God is our refuge encourage you to praise God even in times of trouble?

3. Why do the psalmists link blessedness (happiness) to God's presence?

4. Praise psalms call the community of God to join together in celebration of his attributes and works. How might the local church stir up our desire to praise God?

5. When are you tempted to think God is withholding something good from you? How do praise psalms assure you of God's care and provision?

6. What are some reasons you can praise God today? How would your life change if you started each morning by meditating on these things?

7. What was one thing that convicted, encouraged, instructed, or stood out to you this week?

8. How did these psalms help you turn your eyes to Jesus?

What did you see or learn about Jesus?

What do you need to believe as a result?

How should you live differently?

♪ Hymn for the Week

"Praise to the Lord, the Almighty"

Praise to the Lord, the Almighty, the King of creation!
O my soul, praise him, for he is your health and salvation!
Come, all who hear; now to his temple draw near,
join me in glad adoration.[6]

Additional Psalms of Praise for Further Study

Psalms 8, 47, 48, 67, 68, 95, 100, 105, 135, and 150

We've listed general questions in an appendix that you can use while studying these psalms.

---

6 Joachim Neander, "Praise to the Lord, the Almighty," trans. Catherine Winkworth, 1863, https://hymnary.org.

Appendix

Questions for Studying Additional Psalms

We hope this study is only the beginning of your interaction with the Psalms. At the end of each chapter, we suggested additional psalms to study. Here are some general questions you can use to guide your study of those psalms or any others!

Look for Poetic Devices

- Is there a superscription? If so, how does it inform your understanding of the psalm?
- List repeated words/phrases. What is the psalmist emphasizing?
- Look for parallelism in the psalm. What is the psalmist emphasizing?
- What imagery is used in the psalm? What does the imagery convey?

Look for Context

- Check the cross-references for each verse of the psalm to find related verses in other parts of the Bible. If your Bible doesn't include cross-references, you can use an online version like www.esv.org.
- Does the psalm reference earlier parts of the Bible?
- Is the psalm quoted in other parts of the Bible?
- Read cross-referenced passages and make note of insights that help you understand the psalm you're studying.

Look for Structure

- Is there a chiasm? If so, what is the psalmist emphasizing?
- If there's not a chiasm, or if you're not sure, consider the flow of ideas in the psalm. How does the psalm begin and end? How do the stanzas work together to reveal an emphasis? What do you learn by observing the stanzas?

Look for Christ

- How does this psalm point forward to Christ?
- How is this psalm fulfilled in Christ?

Look for Application

- What is the psalmist's main point? What overall message did the psalmist seek to convey to the original reader of this psalm?
- Consider this psalm's message in light of the gospel. How should you respond to this psalm?
- What two or three actions can you take to align your life more closely with the message of this psalm?

TGC | THE GOSPEL COALITION

The Gospel Coalition (TGC) exists to renew and unify the contemporary church in the ancient gospel by declaring, defending, and applying the good news of Jesus to all of life.

Guided by a Council of more than 40 pastors in the Reformed tradition, TGC seeks to foster a mighty movement of spiritual renewal. We want to see God bless local churches with a gospel-centered ministry that fully integrates corporate worship, expository preaching, joyful obedience to God's Word, effective evangelism, loving community, and faithful engagement in the world.

Through its women's initiatives, TGC aims to equip, connect, and encourage women's ministry leaders and women in local churches globally. We do this through in-person gatherings and by producing resources including Bible studies, articles, podcasts, cohorts, books, and curricula. We support the growth of women in faithfully studying and sharing the Scriptures, in actively loving and serving the church, and in spreading the gospel of Jesus Christ in all their callings.

Join us by visiting TGC.org so you can be equipped to love God with all your heart, soul, mind, and strength, and to love your neighbor as yourself.

TGC.org